Apotheosis

Lord Serious Hakim Allah's Habeas Corpus Appeal

Also available by Lord Serious

The Powerless Pinky is a fun tale that will help children develop a deeper appreciation for their individual self-worth, inspire them to use their natural talents, and cooperate with others. As they will soon learn from the Pinky, regardless of outward appearance, each individual has his or her own purpose in life. People should use their differences to complement one another instead of tear each other down. This is the only path to true peace.

THE POWERLESS PINKY

By Lord Serious

More titles coming soon!

APOTHEOSIS

(Lord Serious Hakim Allah's Habeas Corpus Appeal)

By Lord Serious Hakim Allah, 120°+
Additional Material by Saint Sincere Quintessence Allah, 120°+

Lost Word, Inc

Lost Word, Inc.

1621 Central Avenue

Cheyenne, WY 82001

www.lostwordnation.com

Email: contactlostword@gmail.com

Like us on Facebook: www.facebook.com/lostwordllc

Follow us on Instagram: www.instagram.com/lost_word_llc

ISBN: 978-1-7342202-0-9

DEDICATION

I dedicate this to my elders and ancestors who have returned to the essence. Also, to the True & Living who carry on their legacy of building a better tomorrow for the babies.

"If I have seen further it is by standing on the shoulders of giants." -Issac Newton

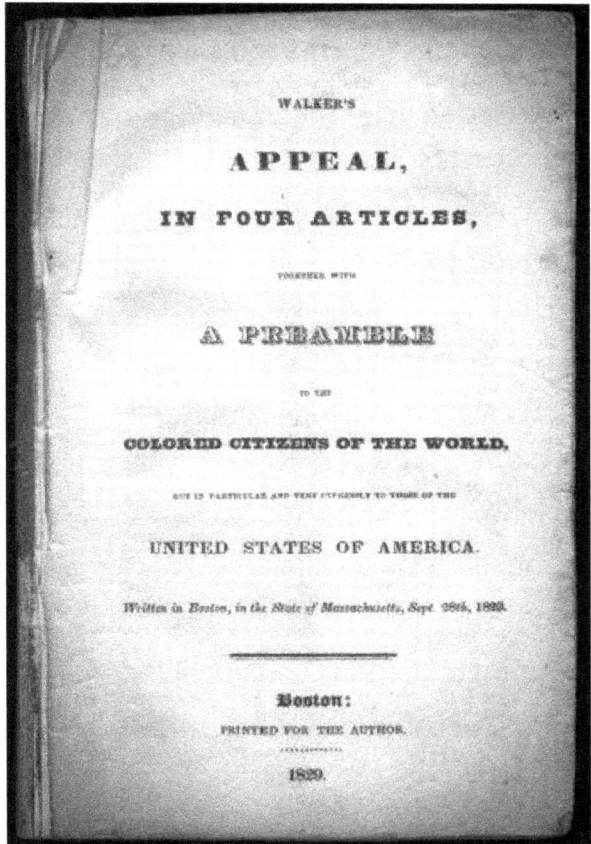

WALKER'S

APPEAL,

IN FOUR ARTICLES,

TOGETHER WITH

A PREAMBLE

TO THE

COLORED CITIZENS OF THE WORLD,

BUT IN PARTICULAR AND VERY EXPRESSLY TO THOSE OF THE

UNITED STATES OF AMERICA.

Written in Boston, in the State of Massachusetts, Sept. 28th, 1829.

Boston:

PRINTED FOR THE AUTHOR.

1829.

Table Of Contents

FOREWORD[1]

by Saint Sincere Quintessence Allah (Q. Jones III) 120°+

"Our problems are man-made therefore, they may be solved by man. And man can be as big as he wants. No problem of human destiny is beyond human beings."
-John F. Kennedy

It is time that we as a people—as Black people—take the time to seriously look at the state of our group. We have a severe habit of avoiding the true problems we face, of seriously turning away from them and towards a symptom that mass-society is more comfortable with addressing. But when one is suffering from cancer, the physician does not give them Pepto-Bismol for their vomiting and send them away. They begin a series of treatments aimed at ridding the body of the disease that has infected it. The cancer we face is a system of White Supremacy and it is malignant. We must decide how much longer we will let it fester, spreading itself cell by cell, turning the body against it's own—our children against each other, our law enforcement against the citizens—before we begin an aggressive course of treatment. And aggressive it must be. If history has taught us anything, it has consistently shown that true power concedes nothing without being forced. Police brutality is but a symptom of a much more debilitating disease. Please, my people, how many more lives must we lose before we gain the confront the true problem? Are we so estranged from our history, our glorious cultures of antiquity, that we truly believe this is the best world we can think up? Do we feel ourselves too inferior to create something better than this? Are we so afraid of losing the crumbs that we have been allowed from Massa's table? What is it that is holding us back? What is it that we are afraid of?

---

[1] Originally published Nov. 24, 2019 (written Nov 2016)
www.lostwordnation.com

I am not a race-baiter or hate monger. I am no demagogue or xenophobe. All of us—black, brown, red, yellow and white; man, woman or any other gender; Christian, Muslim, Jew or other—we would all, all of humanity, benefit from the eradication of White Supremacy. I would like for all of us to join this fight—for it is truly humanity's fight—but first I must speak to my own. I know the struggles of the Black race because I am of it. I experience the reality of being a poor black man in a white man's world each and every day. And as a prisoner now there is more stigma placed upon me. I sincerely believe that Black people, because of our unique relationship with, and proximity to, the heart of the beast, must begin the charge towards a better tomorrow. Artistically, intellectually, culturally, social and politically we must break from the status quo. We cannot continue to perpetuate the same ideas that have been hindering us and expect there to come anything but more of the same. That is the definition of insanity. And from where I sit today, typing this missive, we will fit the diagnosis.

It is not a matter of race-survival. Though talk of genocide may stir more to action, the truth is we, as a race, are not going anywhere soon. If anything, we have proven our ability to endure some of the worst mankind has inflicted upon its own. No, it is not our survival that is at stake; it is our lives. For what is living if one is not living free? What is freedom without equal opportunity? What is equality without justice? The state that we occupy now was not intended for humanity. We live like animals: constantly fearing for our lives, worrying about our next meal, or finding adequate shelter. In such a state what time does one have for love, for culture, for the self-actualization that is the goal of every human being—that transcendental purpose which stirs us to reflect the image and likeness of our Creator? All of us, we strive to live, not simply survive. And we deserve to live. Our children deserve to live.

Let's not get caught up in Kaepernick's stand (or lack thereof) but focus on the issues that caused him to act. and let's not focus on those particular issues but aren't the mentality that breeds them. You must get to the source. If not, we will find ourselves stuck in a constant cycle of cosmetic Reformation that truly gets us nowhere. You fight against slavery then here comes peonage and convict leasing. We fight against them and here comes Jim Crow. We fight against Jim Crow then here comes The war on drugs. Then mass incarceration. Then police shootings. And on and on so forth and so far. As long as we just settle for cutting the heads off this Hydra, more will only continue to rise up; we must stab at the heart of the beast. And we can do it. No problem of man is beyond man's ability. As my brother, Lord Serious, once told me, "Since we are all born with the ability, we all have a responsibility, but where there is no accountability there can be no dependability."

P.E.A.C.E.
POLITICAL
ECONOMIC AND
COMMUNITY
ENGAGEMENT

"Our greatest fear is not that we are inadequate but that we are powerful beyond measure... Your playing small does not serve the world."
-Nelson Mandela, adopted from poet Marianne Williamson

PREFACE

by Lord Serious Hakim Allah

Lord Serious Hakim Allah's Habeas Corpus Appeal is my contribution to the Herculean labor of bolstering the parapet of black resistance against the ceaseless onslaught of White supremacy. The struggle for Black liberation is a protracted one, and the social media posts contained within this book represent a continuum of the abolitionist writings of yesterday. David Walker's Appeal is the cornerstone upon which this keystone rests, and without contributions like his to our common cause, I would lack the guidance from my ancestors from the antebellum period, reconstruction period, Jim Crow period and Civil Rights period. Blacks today must find a way to contend with our period; the mass incarceration of Black men, women, and children.

A century ago W.E.B. Dubois identified the color-line as the biggest problem of his era. This historical fact is indicative that the racial barrier is a problem America is unwilling to solve. Is a hundred years not enough? Would you have us wait a hundred more? Do you suggest that we just keep our heads down and suffer silently while you continue to impede our ability to make forward progress as citizens of the same country our ancestors built during three hundred plus years of forced slave labor. This same country who we fought to liberate from the oppressive British Crown, and in doing so, the first blood to drench the soil to protect the American flag shared the same gene type of those whom your ancestors kidnapped from the shores of Africa and dragged over here in chains. You cannot name one war we have failed to answer your call to arms to defend this country. Yet the blood, sweat and tears my race has deposited towards building a better future for ourselves as your fellow citizens and neighbors, has not provided us with the return that we had hoped for. In fact, history proves that our four hundred years of compliance, accommodation, and cooperation has not only been unappreciated by you, but it was also futile.

The four hundred years of Black acquiescence to the White power structure has gotten us nowhere. Slavery has never been effectively abolished; Blacks are still being subjected to public executions without a fair trial; Blacks are still being exploited and are denied equitable compensation compared to Whites; and Black children are still disproportionately given a substandard education. Too many times Blacks have won the battle only to lose the war at the negotiation table by accepting another Carthaginian Treaty. When the terms of the agreement are so debilitating that it leaves your nation in a worse condition than the one you were already in you have every right to be critical of the leadership that agreed to its terms. Just look at the deceptive wording of the 13th Amendment that permits mass incarceration to exist today. Was this the form of freedom Frederick Douglas intended for us? Analyze the impotence of the Civil Rights Act which is practically an unenforceable piece of legislation that has failed to protect us from the racist White cop, or how the Voting Rights Act, which was supposed to protect the Black ballot from voter suppression has become a nonexistent remedy. Was this the future Martin Luther King Jr. dreamed of?

The integrationist has been duped by the White liberal every step of the way. Thus, it is clear that Blacks should never trust the forked tongue of the White liberal. His promises of a legislative utopia will never manifest. He is a used car salesman selling lemons and his livelihood is dependent upon finding a fool with sore feet and a pocket full of money. The legislative vehicle always breaks down as soon as you drive it about twenty miles down road. And when you take it back to the salesman he tells you the problem is not covered in your warranty. This warranty is full of all sorts of loopholes that you are unaware of. And what makes it worse is that the salesman knew that the radiator would overheat because his conservative mechanic friend wouldn't allow him to sell that vehicle without him being able to get under the hood to tinker with the parts first. This is why I must warn you Caveat Emptor! Which means "Buyer Beware". Black people must beware of what the integrationist buys from the White liberal. I am not suggesting that the Black integrationist has no role to play in the new direction we must lead our people. What I'm saying is that Blacks cannot afford to continue to be divided by partisan politics, we cannot view ourselves as Democrats or Republicans, or take the political stance of integrationist vs. nationalist. Instead let us have enough love for ourselves that we put our race first for a change. And as this Black race moves towards nationhood, we should use the strategies of both integrationist and nationalist to meet the demands of the situation on an as needed basis.

Just think how much further our people would have gotten if Booker T. Washington had united with W.E.B. Dubois? Although this unity did occur between Martin and Elijah Muhammed, and Martin and Malcolm X, the untimely deaths of Malcolm and Martin prevented them from perfecting this new approach. Therefore it is time that our generation pick up where these leaders left off, and our approach to effectuating Black liberation should take the form of a consolidated effort between the integrationist and the nationalist. Let's not lose time arguing over which economic policy is better for Blacks, capitalism or socialism, and let's just build our own economic foundation by using whichever approach produces the best results in the current economic climate. Find out what works in New York? What works in St. Louis? What works in Oakland? What works in Flint Michigan? What works in New Orleans? And what works in Virginia? And then employ those tactics in the environment where they work best. We must be swift and changeable but always remainable; meaning whatever the current conditions are we must possess the adaptability to respond to them while remaining firmly rooted to our common cause; the acquisition of Freedom, Justice, and Equality for our race.

I am neither pro-black or anti-white, I am not anti-government nor am I pro-establishment. I am against no one regardless of race, religion, nationality, creed, or political affiliation. However, if enmity does exist between us, it is because you oppose me speaking truth. If you oppose anyone challenging the social dynamics that keeps Blacks disproportionately poor and oppressed, it is you who is being the racists. I am merely highlighting the facts as they are, and I have over four hundred years of documented evidence to support my claim that White America will never change. The chains, shackles, whips, rapes, beatings, castrations, lynchings, bombings, and shootings are just the beginning of the horrors we've faced. You have subjected us to all sorts of pain: psychological warfare, medical warfare, environmental warfare, biological warfare, and chemical warfare. Any other race of people would have long ago severed all ties with you for the atrocities you have committed against them. Therefore I unequivocally assert that we have every right to resist, we have every right to protest, and we have every right to exercise self-determination in choosing a new direction for our race. Because it is history who is the unbiased friend to humanity. It is history who is the objective accountant of facts. It is history who is the impartial judge, and it is history who calls White America liars, deceivers and fraudulent in its dealings with Blacks all over the world. Who am I to say otherwise? History has shown us how filthy you are in all of your affairs and it has counseled us to run you from amongst us.

Lord Serious Hakim Allah's Habeas Corpus Appeal, is not an appeal to White consciousness seeking contriteness. History has shown us that moral persuasion is an approach that cannot secure long term security for my race, because White America has no morality in its dealings with the non-White world. Men and women far greater than I have tried to reason with you, but you are a savage in the pursuit of happiness and words cannot satisfy your blood lust. Only after you have shed more blood will you grant respite, only after you murder our children will you join us in peaceful protest. Only after you assassinate our leadership will you make legislative concessions. But you are careful enough to ensure that these concessions will never be enough to threaten White privilege in practice. The words within these documents only hold the power to do so in theory alone.

However, where I diverge from David Walker's proposal is that I do not want Blacks to overthrow your government. You can keep that garbage. Instead I want Blacks to rise up and form our own government. We do not have to violate the laws of your constitution because the U.S Constitution authorizes us to do everything we need to do. Every empire will eventually fall, and with President Trump in office, this country has become so divided that Congress couldn't sit down at the table and pass the salt. So in the words of my righteous brother Jesus let us give to Caesar what belongs to Caesar. But what belongs to God let no man try to divide or separate, because God is just as wrathful as he is merciful. And who has been more merciful than the Black man? Who has been more loyal to White America than the Black man? Who has been more patient with White America than the Blacks? But you have plucked our last nerve. You have placed one too many straws on this camel's back. We have run out of patience with you. This is why we will no longer wait for you to do for us, what we have the power to do for ourselves.

For too many years we have allowed our subconscious feelings of inferiority to cause us to underestimate ourselves. During slavery they indoctrinated Blacks to doubt themselves. They told us that they did us a favor by coming to save us from them jungles in Africa. They told us we were a people without law or religion before they forced Christianity down our throats. They told us that after being freed the slaves lacked self-direction and volunteered their services as sharecroppers. Yes, the White man has done an amazing job in telling us lies and programming us to be self-defeating before we even start. When the truth is, we had advanced civilizations with sewage systems while Europeans were throwing feces out of their windows into the streets. The truth is, we had founded mega churches in Egypt, Carthage, and Ethiopia before the Romans got their filthy hands on it, and began using Christianity to shield their dirty religion. The truth is, collectively Black people possess the skills and expertise needed to build and run their own government, and in fact we possess enough love for humanity to establish a form of jurisprudence where our tribunals could even guarantee the alien a just and fair trial. How can I be certain of this you ask? Because we have done it before and it has been prophesied that we shall do it again.

The greatness of our ancestors is written in our genetic code, and the more we get in tune with who we really are as a race of people, the more our innate potential will begin to resurface. For those of us who come from a long line of athletes, something instinctive happens when we step into the arena. For those who come from a long line of musicians, something special occurs when we step on the stage. For those of us who come from a long line of intellectuals, we seem to find ourselves when we get lost in deep thought. The same holds true for our ability to govern ourselves. Do not look at the countries of Africa today and think we are unfit to lead ourselves. You must remember that just like you, these people are also victims of White Supremacy. These people have been conquered, colonized, and are continuously under attack from their colonizer's covert agencies, who interfere with their traditional African democracy by establishing puppet regimes. And when they cannot corrupt the real leadership they will sponsor the opposition party to stage a coup. When this cannot be done then they will just call the leader a dictator and then assassinate him. Compare the quality of life for the Libyan when Gaddafi was ruling, to the chaotic state these people have been reduced to since his death.

Where would Black people in America be if we had followed our nationalist leadership instead of the integrationist? What if we had continued to fight America's separate but equal doctrine in the Black conscious instead of in the courtroom? Would we have continued to build more Black Wall Streets like the township in Tulsa, Oklahoma? What if instead of being nonviolent, we had embraced the militant approach and had an army to defend that community from the White backlash it received from its jealous rural neighbors? What if the schools had never been integrated, would our historical Black colleges been in a position to give Dr. Sebi the institutional support he needed to streamline his cures and herbal remedies, the same way the Tuskegee Institute gave George Washington Carver the support he needed to experiment with the peanut? Why continue to wonder what if? We cannot change the past, but we do not have to continue to make those same mistakes in the future. This is just the beginning of what I have to share with you my beautiful brothers and

sisters. We can love and embrace people of all hues, but let us never love them more than we love our own. This is the natural way of all living things. From ant colonies to blue whales. We can coexist and even cooperate, but self-preservation is the law we all must abide by. Those who advocate Blacks to do otherwise only wish to use us as a tool and also a slave.

P.E.A.C.E
Proper Education Always Corrects Error

Lord Serious Hakim Allah, 120°+

LORD SERIOUS HAKIM ALLAH'S HABEAS CORPUS APPEAL (Part 1)

(Originally published on Facebook on or about August 2016)

In 1828 A.D. a series of articles were published and circulated in the U.S. entitled "David Walker's Appeal". David Walker was born in Wilmington, North Carolina in the year of 1785 A.D.. The cruel and oppressive effects of slavery were felt by most Blacks living in the South at this time, and David Walker was one of the first from amongst the race to gain national notoriety for speaking out against the brutality and abuse. The following is an excerpt of a portion of an article:

"I AM FULLY aware, in making this appeal to my much afflicted and suffering brethren, that I shall not only be assailed by those whose greatest earthly desires are, to keep us in abject ignorance and wretchedness, and who are of the firm conviction that Heaven has designed us and our children to be slaves and beast of burden to them and their children. I say, I do not only expect to be held up to the public as an ignorant, impudent and restless disturber of the public peace, by such avaricious creatures as well as a mover of insubordination - and perhaps put into prison or to death, for giving a superficial exposition of our miseries, and exposing tyrants. But I am persuaded, that many of my brethren, particularly those who are ignorantly with slave - holders or tyrants, who acquire their daily bread by the blood and sweat of their more ignorant brethren - and not a few of those too, who are too ignorant to see beyond their own noses, will rise up and call me cursed - Yea, the jealous ones among us will perhaps use more abject subtlety, by affirming this work is not worth pursuing, that we are well situated, and there is no use in trying to better our condition, for we cannot. I will ask one question here - Can our condition be any worse?"

In 1831 A.D. David Walker died under mysterious circumstances. But even David Walker was aware of the condemnation he would receive from both the oppressed and the oppressor. The fate of the revolutionary is sealed from the moment he or she dedicates their lives to the resistance and liberation of their people. There are two great things that can happen to you - VICTORY or MARTYR ME! It is with this same revolutionary spirit that I pay homage to my ancestor's struggle by carrying on that legacy of resistance in this fight for the liberation of all African descendants by submitting my own Habeas Corpus Appeal.

What you may not understand is that the laws of any country are founded upon the moral foundation of that nation and it is a fact that during David Walker's era slavery was socially acceptable. This moral precedent had long been established in the United States Supreme Court of Public Opinion. After the decision had been reached by White Americans to continue their inhumane treatment toward Blacks, David Walker filed his direct appeal, circulating the above writings and appealing to people's hearts. David Walker's Appeal would inspire many slaves and former slaves alike to take a stand and fight for freedom, justice and equality. However, it failed to arouse the slave revolt he had hoped would bring an end to the institution of slavery.

Today we live in an era where slavery has taken on a new form with the disproportionate mass incarceration of Blacks. Now my race finds itself being chained, shackled, and disenfranchised all over again. I recognize that the very advances many of my ancestors fought, bleed, and died for are now being strippen away under the color of law, and after having exhausted all other remedies, the petition of the Great Writ is now being submitted; the case of America's racism is being brought before the United States Supreme Court of Public Opinion once again, and should this appeal be denied for any reason, our next step as a race of people is to bring our claims against you, to the International Court of Justice and International Criminal Court. We will give all that we have and all within our power to hold you accountable for these crimes against humanity, and force you to answer for your crimes before the entire world! But let us not get too ahead of ourselves, we must exhaust this remedy first. So I need to bring you up to speed on the significance of why I chose to call this Lord Serious Hakim Allah's Habeas Corpus Appeal, and why, it's important to reinterpret David Walker's Appeal for our generation.

Let me first define what the word Habeas Corpus means so that the importance of this document may be fully understood. According to Miriam Webster's Dictionary of Law:

Habeas corpus, n. [Medieval Latin, literally, you should have the body. (The opening words of the writ)]. any of several writs originating at common law that are issued to bring the party before the court.

The founding fathers held this writ in such high esteem that they jealously protected it within their constitution. Here's what that group of geriatric White bigots dressed like the Quaker Oats Man had to say:

The privilege of the Writ of Habeas Corpus shall not be suspended, unless when in Cases of Rebellion or Invasion the public Safety may require it. (U.S. Constitution, Article I, Section 9, Part 2.)

What are the crimes against humanity we are accusing the U.S. of committing? The enslavement and genocide of Blacks. The 13th Amendment states, in pertinent part, "Neither slavery nor involuntary servitude, **EXCEPT AS A PUNISHMENT FOR CRIME** whereof the party shall have been duly convicted, shall exist within the United States, or any place subject to their jurisdiction." (emphasis added) This Amendment was passed in 1865 A.D. after the United States Supreme Court case, Dred Scott v. Sanford, which was decided in

15

1857 A.D.. Chief Justice Taney delivered the following opinion of the Court:"The question is simply this: can a Negro, whose ancestors were imported into this country, and sold as slaves, become a member of the political community formed and brought into existence by the Constitution of the United States, and as such become entitled to all of the rights, and privileges, and immunities guaranteed by that instrument to the citizen?...And this being the only matter in dispute on the pendings, and the court must be understood in this opinion as speaking of that class only, that is, of those persons who are descendants of Africans who were imported into this country, and sold as slaves." (Dred Scott v. Sanford, 60 U.S. 393, 403 (1957).)

What the Court would say next would show that the U.S. Supreme Court is really the lower court, to the United States Supreme Court of Public Opinion.

"It is difficult at this day to realize **THE STATE OF PUBLIC OPINION** in relation to that unfortunate race... But the **PUBLIC HISTORY** of every European nation displays it in a manner too plain to be mistaken. They had...been regarded as beings of an inferior order, and altogether unfit to associate with the white race, either in social or political relations; and so far inferior, that they had no rights which the white man was bound to respect; and that the negro might be justly and lawfully reduced to slavery for his benefit. He was bought and sold, and treated as an ordinary article of merchandise and traffic, whenever a profit could be made by it. **THIS OPINION** was at that time fixed and universal in the civilized portion of the white race. IT WAS **REGARDED AS AN AXIOM IN MORALS AS WELL AS POLITICS,** which no one thought of disputing, or supposed to be open to dispute; and men in every grade and position in society daily and habitually acted upon it in their private pursuits, as well as matters in public concern, without for a moment doubting the correctness of this OPINION." (emphasis added) (Dred Scott v. Sanford, 60 U.S. 393, 407 (1957).)

This ruling only legitimized all of the complaints expressed by David Walker, and proved that every claim he brought before the U.S. Supreme Court of Public Opinion in his 1828 appeal held merit. Therefore the decision of the Court of Public Opinion to deny David Walker's Appeal was an error. Within Lord Serious Hakim Allah's Habeas Corpus Appeal, I have laid out my generation's case against America, and I will show how it was an error on Blacks not to take heed to David Walker's advice, and I will conclude this petition by showing that I am entitled to the relief sought because the U.S. has been unlawfully keeping the political body of Blacks in bondage for 400 years.

My race has been misled and lied to by White America, they have fooled us into believing that the 13th Amendment freed us from slavery. White America has tricked us into believing that they have changed their OPINION about Blacks not being entitled to the same rights, privileges, immunities and constitutional guarantees as them. But in reality there is still a large percentage of White Americans today who still hold Chief Justice Taney's opinion about Black people.

But as the socio-political climate began to change due to the economic shifts brought by the industrial revolution, the abolitionist sentiment of White northerners would prevail, and as a result the 13th Amendment was passed. However, it never abolished slavery in all of its forms; neither was it intended to. The cunning rhetoric of this legal document proves that even the northern Whites were pro-slavery, because they authorized slavery to be enforced as punishment of a crime. The law in the U.S. has always supported the institution of slavery and these laws have always been used to justify the enslavement of members of my race.

For the U.S. to only make up 5% of the world's population, but for it to have the world's highest incarceration rate is no coincidence; this is a **consequence** of Black negligence. From the first group of slaves

17

who were fooled by John Hawkins to board his ship, to the suspect who gets fooled by the White detective to make inculpatory statements against his or her own penal interest. The institution of slavery has only survived because Blacks refuse to stop trusting their enslavers! But our trusting nature is an honorable quality when you are dealing with other honorable people. But history shows that these people are not lovers of humanity, they are a species of humankind who preys upon other humans, and your trusting nature is a weakness when dealing with them.

The enslavement of another human has been universally condemned. Blacks are the minority in this country but the fact that we are being disproportionately incarcerated is prima facie evidence that mass incarceration is just another form of slavery. The fact that White people also are victims to this system means absolutely nothing. Even during the colonial period Whites were forced into indentured servitude by other Whites. The continuity of America's institution of slavery spans four hundred years and, it is in violation of the Universal Declaration of Human Rights, Article 4 which states, "No one shall be held in slavery or servitude; **SLAVERY AND THE SLAVE TRADE SHALL BE PROHIBITED IN ALL THEIR FORMS.**" (emphasis added) I will speak more about the genocide aspect in Part 2. Peace!

LORD SERIOUS HAKIM ALLAH'S HABEAS CORPUS APPEAL (Part 2)
(Originally published on Facebook on or about August 2016)

Peace and blessings to all those worldwide who may be reading these words with a sympathetic heart and a mind full of righteous indignation; for all those who are able to recognize the imminent threat that now opposes our generation today. Yes, the line of demarcation is being drawn again with the intent of further dividing this country along the color barrier, and we cannot afford to pretend like a genocide is not happening. We cannot afford to take the coward's way out, nor should we pretend that race doesn't exist. I am not preaching hate against anyone. But IF you **love yourself**, and IF you **love your kind**, then now is the time to take a proactive approach to ensure the genetic survival of the Black race in America.

For all those who are tired of empty rhetoric that simply highlights problems but never offers any real solutions. For all those who are tired of marching and protesting. For all those who are tired of watching Caucasian police officers murder unarmed Black people showing no regard for human life. If you recognize that today is a new era of time now, and that the tactics of the Civil Rights movement are outdated and out of touch; but are unsure about what role you can play in trailblazing a different path for our people's revolution: listen carefully to what I am about to say, because I am about to instruct you on what **MUST** be done!

Random House Webster's Unabridged Dictionary defines genocide as:

genocide, n. the deliberate and systematic extermination of a national, racial, political, or cultural group.

It has now become clear to the Black man in America what he is up against. The Sean Bell murder left many of us scratching our heads in the early 2000's, but many within my generation were fooled into believing it was an isolated incident. The Trayvon Martin shooting left us all angered, but once again, we gave you the benefit of the doubt. Michael

Victims of Police Brutality

Brown, Eric Garner, Freddy Grey, and the many others in between, who I have not named, left us outraged until that frustration boiled over into riots that shook the nation; as we demanded your attention so that we could begin a national conversation. But with the tragic deaths of two more Black men at the hands of White police officers, the reality we face in this country can no longer be denied. This is an attempt to systematically wipe us out!

Before I get into what we must do to change course, I will first tell you what you can expect to happen in the next 12 months in the aftermath of the Alton Sterling and Philando Castile "murders":

1) There will be protest with people of all races;
2) There will be a host of political debates composed of multiracial panels;
3) There will be Black leadership who calls for calm;
4) There will be Black attorneys who swear up and down a Civil Rights violation has occured, and they will sound so convincing you will have little doubt that these police officers will finally be held accountable;
5) The state or Feds will investigate;
6) A Grand Jury will be held, and most likely, no indictments will be

brought against the police officers who both were practically caught on camera!;
7) You probably won't believe me until it actually happens;

When things do go exactly as I predicted this will prove:

1) Protesting and marching alone will never be enough to change the White power structure's perception on why #BlackLivesMatter;
2) That, the debates and panels are shams. Those panels are not all inclusive and until they begin routinely inviting grassroots leaders and allow these community leaders to express their views, the conversations are purely intellectual. Negotiations cannot occur until they start inviting the real leadership to the table;
3) That, the White power structure has always appointed Black leadership for the sole purpose of maintaining their control over our people;
4) That, just like those leaders (above) these attorneys have an invested interest in maintaining the current system; if these attorneys really wanted to bring these atrocities to a stop they would aid us in bringing the U.S. before the International Courts for their human rights violations;
5) Both state and Federal law enforcement agencies know that a conviction for police misconduct is easier to get in the state, because state legislation gives prosecutors more variety in the amount of charges they can bring against the police. However, many states' penal codes are ambiguous (unclear) on what extent deadly force is authorized, and unless the police department has a policy to clarify these ambiguities it becomes even more difficult to secure a Grand Jury indictment against an offending officer. But if the Feds do pick up the case the wording of the Civil Rights Act basically makes it unenforceable. It must be shown beyond a reasonable doubt that the officer had a "specific intent" to violate the deceased person's constitutional rights;
6) None of us ever know who these people are who serve on the

Grand Jury. At least in open court the public is permitted to sit in attendance during the selection of the petit jury; and because there is no transparency, we have every right to be suspicious of the process. Whoever these people are, they seem to have an invested interest in maintaining the status quo, because they always find a way to nullify our ability to indict. When this happens in the case of Mr. Sterling and Mr. Castile, it will prove that the political analyst, Black political leaders, and the Black attorneys LIED to you when they told you that placing body cameras on White rogue police officers would deter them from continuing to shoot unarmed or cooperating Black people;

7) By the time we reach this point more innocent Black lives will be lost due to this same problem.

Now this is what we MUST do to prevent our race from being systematically wiped out. Let us learn to exercise community control. Let us learn to govern ourselves. Let the deaths of Mr. Sterling and Mr.Castile be the last straw. Let us show the world that we are within our natural God given right to exercise self-determination from this day forward. And that, because the Criminal Justice System has been so unjust in its dealings with the Black man in America, make it known to the world that the legitimacy of this institution now is in question. And rather than continuing our practice of being a reactionary people, let us learn the wisdom of what it's like when our people take a proactive approach when addressing our issues with this government.

We should follow the examples set by all those Grand Juries who failed to indict the rogue police officers killing our sons and fathers. You fail to realize just how powerful you are as a tax paying citizen. You have the right to vote. But you also have the civic duty to perform jury duty when called upon to do so. Black leadership continues to educate us on the importance of exercising our right to cast a ballot. But little has been said about jury duty. Although I know you dread the thought of spending your day in the courthouse all day, you should take these words into consideration. You have a habit of weaseling your way out of performing jury duty. You concoct all sorts of excuses for why you cannot serve. But what if our elders and ancestors came up with excuses for why they could not march or perform sit-ins? This is a new era of time now, and because the form of oppression has evolved, in our political and civil disobedience demonstrations we must also evolve.

If you are dissatisfied with the disproportionate arrests and convictions of Black people, and you wish to express your disdain for the system by protesting, then sacrifice your time by serving on every criminal jury you can. During voir dire (questioning of the jury pool) do not seem too eager to serve, because prosecutors will strike you and prevent you from serving. Remain composed during examination, and try to make yourself appear as objective and impartial as possible. Give each side the impression you will give each side a fair trial. And if you are selected as a member of the jury, DO NOT TELL ANYONE WHAT YOU ARE UP TO! It is important that you follow this instruction, do not even tell me. Take this secret to the grave. Now when the case gets brought to the jury for deliberations, follow the examples set by those Grand Juries who judged the police, and nullify every indictment they put in front of you. Don't give any of your fellow jurymen any indication about what you are up to, it's none of their business, and it's your constitutional right to protest. If the majority of the jury say "Guilty" you say "Not Guilty!" If they say "Not Guilty" you can say "Not Guilty" too; this will acquit the defendant, allowing them to walk free just like the police; or, you can say "Guilty", and cost the government money by causing a hung jury. I am encouraging you to do this regardless of the defendant's race or social status. Also employ this tactic regardless of the crime they have been accused of. I know it will be difficult to do when the evidence of guilt is overwhelming. But just remind yourself that there is also video footage of these police murdering unarmed Blacks, so you are only balancing the scales of justice in this corrupt system. This is how we must fight back.

Since we cannot trust this corrupt system, we need to establish People Tribunals or Tribal Courts within our communities. We should democratically select members in our community who have reputations of being fair, just, and morally sound. These individuals should be appointed to arbitrate our affairs whenever disputes arise amongst us and the parties involved cannot resolve the issue on their own. By doing this we will be establishing a culture of accountability back within our villages/communities. When the elders and the youth know that they each will receive a fair hearing, people will be less inclined to take matters into their own hands or resort to using violence.

Furthermore, once the village legitimizes these tribunals through their participation and adherence to its rulings, we will then expand our jurisdiction. Thus, the next time an alien White cop assaults or murders a member of our village, we will hold our own trial to determine whether the officer's actions were justified or not. If this foreigner refuses to answer the subpoena to appear before our court then we will hold their trial in absentia (absence). That decision will represent the voice our community, and when the community has spoken the members of the village will enforce that ruling on whomever.

Next we must formulate a security force to protect our village from domestic and foreign threats. This security force should be equipped with camera-equipped drones to patrol the village's airspace and maintain a visual on all police vehicles that enter our village at all times. This camera footage should be on a live feed that can be viewed by the public over the internet whenever it is observing the police. The men and women on this security force should be knowledgeable of U.S. law. Whenever a member of our village is being detained by police for any reason, they should be dispatched to the scene not to antagonise the cops, but to inform members of our village what their rights are.

And in cases where we must defend our community, we have no other choice but to arm ourselves. Use whatever weapon you are most comfortable with; if love is your weapon then love your village enough to fight for its people. Use your fist, teeth and nails if that's all you have. Use your walking stick or cane if that's all you can carry. Use poles, pipes, chains and bats. Use knives, daggers, machetes or swords. Use crossbows, bow and arrows, handguns, shotguns, high powered rifles, and slingshots! However you choose to arm yourself, just let it be lawful. The Black nationalist does not use the image of the gun to instigate a race war. Black nationalist use the image of the gun as a deterrent. Furthermore, the U.S. has more gun violence than any other nation in the world. Gun violence is another example of a problem that White America is unwilling to fix. So the Black nationalist will motivate you to fix it by arming every Black household, and because we know you don't want guns in the hands of your Black slaves, the Black integrationist is relieved to know that this will get you to pass some laws. The Black nationalist will force White America to do a better job of regulating gun control, and because all of the major gun manufacturers are complicit in this negligence, White America, do not be surprised when every village purchases a 3D printer and begins to manufacture their own guns and rifles. There is no law to prohibit them from doing this, neither is there any law to prohibit them from carrying this weapon in public.

If the U.S. government really wanted to stop gun violence, they would pass legislation to force the manufacturers to put thumbprint safety locks on every new firearm sold. This would prevent depressed White kids from stealing their parents guns and then using them to massacre other school children in the cafeteria whenever they get angry. This will prevent guns from being sold illegally, and if the firearm is resold, the new buyer would have to go through the proper government or industry channels to get their thumb print recognized by the safety lock's system. Many of you reading this are currently using more advanced technology to unlock your smart phones. I do not hate anybody; I am pro-righteousness and anti-devilishment. You cannot have a righteous nation without law and order, and it is the devil's job to get the wrong doers. Black people cannot beat the White race in wickedness, the only way to overcome them is through uniting in righteousness.

In this series of writings entitled Lord Serious Hakim Allah's Habeas Corpus Appeal, I am giving you new strategies from the Black integrationist philosophy of nonviolence and civil disobedience, and showing you how it can work in unison with the militant "by any means necessary" philosophy of the Black nationalist. Education is the necessary means through which our people shall achieve liberation. Thus, if we hope to overcome the oppression and the suffering being inflicted upon Blacks, we must learn from men like David Walker, and learn to take heed to the wisdom of these words:

"When we take a retrospective view of the arts and sciences - the wise legislators - the Pyramids, and other magnificent buildings - the turning of the channel of the river Nile, by the sons of Africa or of Ham, whom among learning originated, and was carried thence into Greece, where it was improved upon and refined. Thence among the Romans, and all over the then enlightened parts of the world, and it has been enlightening the dark and benighted minds of men from then, down to this day. I say, when I view retrospectively, the renown of that once mighty people, the children of our great progenitor I am indeed cheered. Yea further, when I view that mighty son of Africa, Hannibal, one of the greatest generals of antiquity, who defeated and cut off so many white Romans or murderers, who carried his victorious arms, to the very gate of Rome, and I give it as my candid opinion, that had Carthage been well united and had given him good support, he would have carried that cruel and barbarous city by storm, but they were dis-united, as the coloured people are now, in the United States of America, the reason our natural enemies are enabled to keep their feet on our throats."

LORD SERIOUS HAKIM ALLAH'S HABEAS CORPUS APPEAL (Part 3)

(Originally published on Facebook on or about August 2016)

If while watching the Olympics, you experienced unease or had difficulty with feeling patriotic, this is understandable. If like the crowd in Rio during the beach volleyball tournament you had an urge to publicly boo the U.S., or you secretly rooted for the Black, Brown and Yellow people from around the world whenever they competed against the U.S.; do not feel ashamed, this is all normative behavior for people in our circumstances. It is the U.S. government who should feel ashamed, because they have forced an entire demographic of American citizens to openly question their government's loyalty to them. After witnessing this government marginalize and then exterminate your kind, you are finally realizing that Black people in America do not have the luxury of being patriotic.

I have been informed by my numerous supporters who post these builds on their Facebook pages, that social media may not be the best platform for this type of writing. I am told that the most effective writing formats on social media are short and concise messages. However, our circumstances demand a response, and the solutions to address the many problems plaguing Black people, cannot be summed up in a seven sentence elevator speech. It's time that we have an open and honest dialogue amongst ourselves about what must be done, and this discussion MUST contain a step-by-step analysis to instruct our people on how to effectively carry this plan out. I fully understand my role in our people's struggle at this stage. The question is do you, the reader, understand your role?

When I look at my circumstances as a slave or prisoner from a historical context, the duty of the prisoner has been to utilize their time in confinement developing strategies and tactics to liberate his people, and then share his knowledge with people like you. Yes, I am placing these thoughts into your care, and I am entrusting you to test these theories out, and discover what works in your village and learn what doesn't work. I recognize that it is people like you who hold the true power to change the conditions of your community. I am not writing this because I believe it will attract the attention of the entire Facebook universe. I know exactly who my target audience is, and it is because I understand the mathematical importance of allowing social change and behavior modification to complete every step of the process, I am reaching out to the avant-garde or what I like to call the 5% within the 5%.

Innovators like you in society are a minority in the world's population simply because you are brave enough to think outside of the box. I was not surprised to hear that very few people were willing to read lengthy messages on Facebook. We know that the readers are the leaders, so I am speaking to the present and future community leaders, political activists, and the grassroots and nonprofits. All those with a healthy work ethic, strong will, and who are good teachers, but who may lack fresh and new innovative ideas.

I trust that after analyzing this you will be flexible in your approach when figuring out how best to implement these ideas in your village. These writings are to be used as guidepost, instructing you on what has happened in the past, and how we can protect ourselves and prevent these same abuses from continuing to occur in the future . I do not expect us to agree on everything, this is why I am instructing both integrationist and nationalist. So what you do agree with, it is your responsibility to put it into action the best way you can. If you do your part and I continue to do mine, diffusion will occur. I am not appealing to the majority, because the majority will only understand the significance of these words after they observe you put them into action. Whenever the innovator or risk-taker does something that is unorthodox and it benefits the whole village, then the masses will rally behind that cause and support that individual. After observing and participating, the masses will then begin implementing these changes into their own lives. If you wish to end the self-destructive behavior being displayed in your village then its important that you understand this psychology.

In Part 2, I gave a blueprint on how we as a community can successfully combat police brutality and the disparities in America's Criminal Justice System. I also informed you on what we should expect in the aftermath of the police shootings that occurred in Louisiana and Minnesota. Here's a reminder:

1) There will be protest with people of all races;
2) There will be a host of political debates composes of multiracial panels;
3) There will be Black leadership who calls for calm;
4) There will be Black attorneys who swear up and down a Civil Rights violation has occured;
5) The state or Feds will investigate;
6) A Grand Jury will be held and most likely no indictments will be brought against the police officers who both were practically caught on camera!;
7) You probably won't believe me until it actually happens;

When things do go exactly as I predicted this will prove:

1) Protesting and marching alone will never be enough to change the White power structure's perception on why #BlackLivesMatter;
2) That the debates and panels are shams. Those panels are not all inclusive and until they begin routinely inviting grassroots leaders, and allow these community leaders to express their views, the conversations are purely intellectual. Negotiations cannot occur until they start inviting the real leadership to the table;
3) That the White power structure has always appointed Black

leadership for the sole purpose of maintaining their control over our people;

4) That just like those leaders (above) these attorneys have an invested interest in maintaining the current system;

5) That the Civil Rights movement won the battle but lost the war at the negotiation table, because it has been shown that the Civil Rights Act is unenforceable;

6) We are within our rights to be suspicious of the Grand Jury proceedings due to its culture of non-compliance when it comes to holding the police accountable and the lack of transparency;

But here's the most important point:

7) BY THE TIME WE REACH THIS POINT MORE INNOCENT BLACK LIVES WILL BE LOST DUE TO THE SAME PROBLEM;

With the recent death of a mother and the wounding of a child due to police brutality, and the subsequent death of another Black man in Milwaukee (Sylville Smith) shows and proves the severity of the problem facing us today. Someone needs to put pressure on the Federal Bureau of Investigations to keep track of all victims of police shootings, the same way they keep track of all other crimes. My reasoning for this is because, these police shootings are our generation's equivalent to the unlawful lynchings of Black men during the 19th and early 20th Century. The only way to force the federal government to intervene and take the necessary actions needed to put an end to these atrocities, is to develop a record. This data can dispel the myth that these shootings are just isolated events. A record will prevent the federal government from using plausible deniability as an affirmative defense.

This record will force the Attorney General and Congress to act or risk being held liable for deliberate indifference in the International Courts. This record will force the U.S. to admit that these shootings are symptoms of its culture of systemic racism, and that this racist mentality is a blood sucking parasite using the civil servant as its host. The integrationist should articulate his morally persuasive argument to the White race in this similitude. And when the war cry of the militant nationalist commands Blacks to arm themselves and shoot back, the looming threat of "or else" will compel the oppressor to accommodate the modest request of the integrationist. If not, then the U.S. will soon learn that the militant wasn't making empty threats, he was exercising diplomacy by giving you a warning. Even a blind man can see that if something isn't done to stop these police shootings, they will only result in making the job of the "good cop" more dangerous and difficult.

It is because Ida B. Wells had the statistics on lynchings that she was able to show how widespread and rampant these isolated cases really were. This data helped her change the public opinion about whether these homicides were justified. Ida B. Wells used the facts to raise awareness in the North about the severity of the lynching problem in the South. Ida B. Wells was a militant, but she also understood the importance of diffusion. As a result, she was able to get lynch mob legislation passed to prohibit rogue White males from using their hatred for Black males, as a lawful excuse, to take the law into their own hands and execute Black men in the streets. She understood her role as a member of the avant-garde or what I call the 5% within the 5%. Today's generation of leaders must understand their responsibility, and how the problems our race faced in times past can give us much needed insight on how we can solve the problems we face today. If this is your first time reading Lord Serious Hakim Allah's Habeas Corpus Appeal, I encourage you to search your Friend's timeline and read the two posts that preceded this one. Our fate as a race of people is in your hands, you must carry on the legacy of our ancestors to make the world a better place for the babies. Peace and love!

LORD SERIOUS HAKIM ALLAH'S HABEAS CORPUS APPEAL (Part 4)

(Originally published on Facebook on or about September 2016)

Economic boycotts are an effective tool when utilized properly. However, the call to boycott the film The Birth Of A Nation is unwise. Let me be clear, I do not support the idea that it is okay for any man to take away a woman's right to say "no", even if the man is her husband. This is my personal view on rape. Now as it concerns Nate Parker as an actor and writer, here are a few things we should consider:

1) Mr. Parker has already been paid, the distributor paid him when they brought the rights to the film which allows them to now released the movie in theaters;
2) Like it or not he was never convicted; and
3) **WHY WASN'T THERE SUCH A STRONG PUSH TO BOYCOTT The Great Debaters?**

Now let's analyze that third point. Mr. Parker played a major supporting role in that film starring Denziel Washington. Yet, it appears as though any murmurs of Mr. Parker's questionable past were overshadowed by Denziel's star power. But I think that outlook over simplifies the issue at hand. I do not know the details of the situation, therefore, I cannot speak on that case. My opinion on the matter is strictly being directed to the public response and the smoke screen that is being used to confuse and distract Black people away from the truth. It is true that America has always been a male driven society, that has been repressive and insensitive towards women's rights. It is no coincidence that the 15th Amendment (giving Black men the right to vote - 1870) was passed before the 19th Amendment (which gave women the right to vote - 1920). This is why America would elect a Black man to be its President (Barack Obama, 2008), before a woman would even get nominated as a major political party's frontrunner for the same position (Hillary Clinton, 2016).

However, let us not be easily led in the wrong direction by believing on face value, that a boycott against The Birth Of A Nation, will be in the best interest of Black people, or that it will further the struggle for women's rights. Although a successful boycott would be a moral victory for women's rights, it would be a blow to the head for Black people (Black women included) keeping them unconscious. The media paid little attention to Nate Parker's past while promoting the film The Great Debaters, because the message of that film supported the American puritan value system. Which is the belief, regardless of your social status, IF you work hard in life you will be successful! This is the type of imagery that keeps impoverished Black people docile and submissive to the current power structure. Which allows the rich to continue to generate revenue off of our backs by giving us a false sense of hope. Hope is the carrot the lazy farmer ties to the end of a stick to trick his overworked mule into continuing to plow his bountiful field. This false sense of hope has kept Blacks suffering peaceably for four hundred years.

The Great Debaters posed no threat, nor did it challenge the social standards of its time. It was a mere cinematic novelty that displayed the intellectual acumen of a group of rural Black kids. Whites made money while employing Black actors, and Black audiences walked away feeling inspired. The Great Debaters was an even tradeoff in that regard. But the film had little, to no impact, in altering the lopsided scales of a society that oppresses Black people. However, if you contrast that with the message Black people will receive after watching the life story of Nat Turner in the film The Birth Of A Nation. These two messages couldn't be further apart. Nat Turner's story will leave Black audiences convinced that White America's promise of a fully integrated society, where we are all equal regardless of hue, is just another fairy tale. And that this dream is real as the tooth fairy, a magical being, who will leave money underneath our pillow on the day when the Black man finally does awaken from such child like naveté.

Someone was afraid that our indignation for this so-called free society after watching such powerful imagery, would awaken our African warrior spirit, and motivate us to collectively resist the effects of White Supremacy. Someone was afraid that this recalcitrant spirit would awaken our generation and cause us to rise up and birth a new nation. A new nation of Blacks, who though they were born in America, they no longer identify with it. A new generation of Blacks who will no longer seek to befriend the White majority or plead with them for racial equality. A new nation of Blacks who will not be pacified with aid, support, housing or any other form of slave rations. Someone is afraid that our generation will be the Blacks who will give birth to a new nation through the exercise of self-determination!

Black women, don't boycott The Birth Of A Nation. Black women, take your sons and daughters to see The Birth Of A Nation, and let them see their people's history of resistance to White supremacy. Black women, drag your husbands or boyfriends to see the movie so that they will see what real Black manhood looks like! And at its conclusion, educate that man and your children, so that they may finally understand that our nation can never rise, until Black men stop killing each other and join forces against the real enemy. Teach them that our nation's survival is dependent upon our men being courageous enough to stand up against the injustice being committed against his women and children, and that he must be willing to protect them with his life. Look him in his eyes, and tell that brother you would rather see him die like a man, than live like a coward; and if he refuses, sister, get you another man.

Nat Turner's rebellion was not just a response to David Walker's Appeal. Nat Turner's rebellion was the Minority Opinion of the Court.

Nat Turner's rebellion showed that he agreed with David Walker's Appeal when it stated:

"O! that the coloured people were long since like Moses's excellent disposition, instead of courting favour with, and telling news and lies to our natural enemies, against each other - aiding them in keeping their hellish chains of slavery upon us. Would we not long before this time been respectable men, instead of such wretched victims of oppression as we are? Would they be able to drag our mothers, our fathers, our wives, our children and ourselves, around the world in chains and handcuffs as they do...This question, my brethren, I leave for you to digest. And may God Almighty force it home to your hearts..."

We will now address the pivotal question of what role should athletes and entertainers play in furthering the struggle for Black liberation? Many of the images being portrayed in mass media serve the purpose of reinforcing stigmas and stereotypes of Black dejection and ineptitude. However, images like Nat Turner's rebellion will challenge those ideals of Black helplessness. I've heard that there is a meme showing a group of wealthy White bigots playing a game of monopoly on the backs of Black slaves, and the caption underneath the image says, "All we have to do is stand up and their little game is over!" Locate that meme and share it. But the point I'm making is that imagery is a very powerful tool.

Take for instance, the image of Colin Kaepernick refusing to stand during the National Anthem, and taking a knee in protest against the American flag. Ironically, sitting down has become the new way to stand up. The WNBA players wearing Black Lives Matter T-shirts, is the new way to stand up. NBA players wearing black hoodies, is the new way to stand up. Jada Pinkett-Smith boycotting the Oscars, is the new way to stand up. No, they aren't doing it the same way Muhammad Ali or Paul Robeson did it. However, who's to say that this new method will be less effective than the former? If we should seek to become radicalized at all, let it be for the sake of results and not style.

If the changes we seek are long term changes and not just temporary concessions, then we must recognize that standing up consists of more than just standing on two feet (speaking out). You are still not standing properly if you find yourself still hunched over (economically dependent). Standing up entails that your posture is perpendicular to the Earth below, with your feet planted firmly on the square. This means that your back is straight and your chin is held high (pride and self-esteem gained by being self-sufficient). As long as we continue to be hunched over, they may continue their little game on our backs. But the moment we unite in standing upright on our own two feet, no one can exploit us, because we will be standing on our own economic foundation.

When Black athletes and entertainers truly get fed up with the system, they will no longer accept their role of being the chattel property of bigots like Donald Sterling. They will no longer seek their

37

oppressor's validation of their talents with trophies or accolades. I'm not knocking how they make their living but real changes require real sacrifices. The same way they will accept a pay cut to play for a championship caliber team, when they become 100% dissatisfied they'll sacrifice some of their coins to pool their resources with other dissatisfied athletes, and start their own league and industries to challenge the White monopoly. Jada wasn't the only person in Hollywood who felt that way. Chris Paul didn't look too pleased to put on that Clippers jersey when Sterling's tape came out. Kaepernick wasn't the only NFL player protesting. Who's stopping these multimillionaires from pooling their resources together to form their own industry or league? This would be the reemergence of Black Wall Street. This would signal the resurrection of the Cushite Empire. The only way for Blacks to topple the tyranny of the White Supremacy, is to make the transition from being a nation of consumers, and become a nation of producers. But we need our own industries to accomplish this. Though our athletes and entertainers are making a noble contribution to the struggle for Black liberation, I am afraid what has been done thus far will not be enough. The next generation of Black athletes and entertainers will have to suffer the same hardships unless we put an end to it right now.

If you did not know, I am a slave in the Virginia Department of Corrections (Corruptions). I am not a prisoner, I am a slave because I am Black and I have been "duly convicted" of a crime. Yes, I am one of many Black men who have fallen victim to the 13th Amendment's exception clause. I consciously use the word slave instead of prisoner, or inmate, or offender, or even convict because these words though shameful; they are way too conservative. Black people can accept these titles without cringing. But the truth has always had a distinct ring to it. Truth makes you uncomfortable when you're living a lie, and the truth is I am a slave. I am not a slave to my emotions, my passions, or my desires, no, I am a slave to the Commonwealth of Virginia, where it all started in 1619. This not only brings it full circle, it also makes it four hundred years on the head that this state has been enslaving people who look like me. Harriet Tubman said that she freed three hundred people on her underground railroad without losing one passenger, and she would have freed three hundred more but they didn't know that they were slaves. Nate Parker has expressed remorse and if sincere, Blacks should allow him to redeem himself by making films that will continue to combat the stereotypical images of Blacks. The images in The Birth Of A Nation can awaken the consciousness of many brothers in here with me in ways our words never will. This film may not just redeem Nate Parker, it could potentially redeem every Black man who has contributed to the belief that Black manhood will never resurrect itself, myself included. Peace!

ADDENDUMS

SCHOOL TO PRISON PIPELINE

The social landscape within the U.S. has always been a field of diversity. However, due to a long history of discriminatory practices, not all flora grows and flourishes at the same rate. Instead, the beauty of the minority has been disproportionately choked out by the weeds of racism, classism, and bigotry. To prune the growth of adults as their branches ascend the social strata is one thing, but to completely uproot the youth as their seed of potential is just beginning to sprout is an intolerable offense. Thus, the school to prison pipeline is more than just an eye sore, it is also a condemned structure that is contaminating the field of opportunity for minorities in the U.S., and therefore, it must be removed.

Pedology is both the science and study of soils, and the science and study of the nature and development of children. However, when it comes to cultivating the minds of Black children, the American public school system is intentionally producing a bad yield. Teachers and administrators have created an environment that normalizes discriminatory practices against Black children. Theoretically, all children are given an equal opportunity to receive a primary and secondary education but in practice, Black children are being systematically deprived of their ability to learn by being kept out of classrooms due to the disproportionate enforcement of zero tolerance policies.

Regardless of what the letter of the law says, the truth of the matter is this: the practice of depriving Black children of a quality education has always been the policy of this society since its inception. Frederick Douglass relayed the story of how his enslaver reacted when he discovered that his wife had been teaching him the alphabet. According to Frederick Douglass his enslaver thought an education would ruin him because he would no longer be fit to be a slave.

It goes against the interest of the ruling class to teach the children of their subjects how to compete with their own children whom they plan to leave their inheritance. Therefore, why are Blacks so shocked to discover that there are still members of the White majority who wish to maintain their dominance over the American culture? And why do we seem to be surprised at the extent they are willing to go to while protecting White privilege? This is as much of a dissection of the subversion of the White majority, as it is a constructive critique of Blacks for not taking the necessary precautions to defend themselves against discrimination. I do not expect bigots and racists to become altruistic, nor do I expect our defenses to be impregnable at this stage. But I do expect all of humanity to be wise enough to understand the importance of having their own sentinel. How many times must we get betrayed before we realize that the responsibility of protecting Black children from abuse is exclusively the responsibility of those who are Black alone?

No legislation will ever be enough to protect us from human nature. Within every society friction exists between the majority and the minority, the haves and the have nots. Why?—because they have conflicting interests that place them in competition with the other. We have benefitted from the passages of two constitutional amendments, and multiple Civil Rights Acts; yet, Whites continue to find new and innovative ways to break the law and place Blacks at a disadvantage. When will we graduate from being the helpless nation within a nation and become the nation in a state of pupilage within this nation? If Blacks adopted this perspective they would not be immune to the subversion of Whites, but we would be in a better position to counter it. Our sentinels would reevaluate all legislation that theoretically protects minorities from the discriminatory practices of the White majority—seeking to find all loopholes—and instead of marching and protesting 20 years later when the inevitable happens, Blacks should push their Congressmen and Senators to close those loopholes now.

As a voice of my generation, it is my duty to be critical of the failings of my predecessors. Not to imply that I could have done their jobs better than them, because I have the benefit of hindsight, and I do not live in their era. Therefore, I am not pretending to be a Civil Rights leader. However, if those Civil Rights leaders had been better sentinels they would have recognized that Civil Rights legislation still left Blacks vulnerable. This conclusion could've been reached by analyzing the history of our nation's education system and the competitive nature of the White majority. Just as professional athletes will cheat and use performance enhancing drugs to gain a competitive advantage in the sports world, the desire to gain a competitive edge in economics and politics is an even greater temptation, simply because, there is a lot more at stake. The winner gains more than a trophy, and the loser will have a lot more than just their pride hurt. So, if we are being honest, not being vigilant in standing guard to ensure we would not be cheated was an inexcusable oversight.

Many of us view the public education system as a bedrock institution of our society. This may be true today, but this was not always the case. The state government was not always responsible for providing primary and secondary education to our children. At one time teachers received their wages directly from the parents of the children whom they were educating. This means that there was no public school system in place, and because schools were private institutions there were many American children whose parents couldn't afford to send them to school. Instead the children of these low income families were forced to find employment just to keep their families from starving. So even if they had the option of attending school, many of these families may have found it to be too much of a sacrifice and impractical for their living situation. However, child labor laws would soon remove children from the workforce, and thanks to the states forming the public education system these children soon became students.

This historical analysis reveals two things: the first is that, the children of the elite are the only children guaranteed a quality education in this society, because they are expected to inherit the rulership of the society from their parents. The second is that, the hardships of poverty have a tendency to force children to join the workforce in an effort to provide supplemental income for their struggling families. Initially, the fight for Civil Rights as it pertained to the education system was a challenge to the first issue. Civil Rights leaders were attempting to dismantle a structural defect within the social landscape of the U.S.. However, what began as a challenge to the disparity between the quality of education America's children were receiving, was redefined in a way that totally avoided the root of the problem, and instead focused on its symptoms: the lawfulness of state statutes prohibiting Black children from sharing classrooms with their White counterparts.

After being victorious in their misdirected pursuit, our leadership failed to fortify and protect the advances gained by having the issue of how can we guarantee that Black children receive a quality education, equivalent to the education received by the children of the White elite. Second, they should have taken precautions to resist the likelihood of having poor Black children drop out of school due to the discriminatory practices of White teachers/administrators who may be racists or bigots. Who may I add, never would have taught them if not for integration. After having their academic aspirations derailed and having no legitimate economic opportunities, the only practical alternative to alleviate some of their family's financial hardship naturally pushes these children into a life of crime.

To bring an end to the school to prison pipeline, I think we must address these two issues: how can we guarantee Black children receive a quality education equivalent to the education received by the children of the elite; and how do we prevent our impoverished children from losing faith in the education system and becoming illegitimate capitalist (criminals)? I think we must look at the pre-integration period for clues. More important than the past transgressions of White adults against Black children, is the way Black adults responded. Black communities would pool resources when they had to, or pay individually, out of pocket, to compensate an educated Black to teach their children. These Black teachers shared a common interest with the parents in wanting to see these children succeed academically. This was something positive and therefore we should preserve this. Next, what segregation did was force Blacks to build their own educational institutions. This was the era that gave birth to Historical Black Colleges and Universities (HBCUs). But these Black Colleges and Universities would not have been possible if it were not for private primary and secondary schools were Black youth were encouraged to study and learn so that they could contribute to the accomplishments of their race. This also was positive and therefore deserves preservation.

Our children feeling pressured to drop out of primary or secondary school due to economic hardship was a problem many Blacks faced during that time period as well. Obviously, it isn't going anywhere, so for us to pretend that it doesn't exist, leaves us vulnerable and exposes a weakness that can, and will, continue to be used to disadvantage us further if we do not address it. At one time poverty forced many Black children out of classrooms and into the fields of sharecroppers or into assembly lines. However, due to child labor laws deterring employers from hiring underage children, our children today still face the same financial difficulties. But now their only alternative forces them out of the classrooms and into the streets.

In conclusion, Blacks have the ability to overcome both of the above-mentioned issues by removing their children from public schools and forming, or enrolling their children into, private schools or charter schools where the teachers and administrators look like them. I am aware that not every community has the resources or qualified personnel on hand to make this a reality immediately. Nor, do I believe that just because something is Black that this means the quality will be better. In fact, there are many predominantly Black public schools with high dropout rates and who lack accreditation. This is shameful and will be brought to an end if my advice is followed. All children love to learn. But that love for schooling will disappear in any child whenever attending school feels more like a punishment than it does an opportunity to succeed in life. What I am proposing is that we begin doing whatever is necessary to move toward this being a possibility. In communities where this can be achieved immediately, we should move out on it wholeheartedly, and should the performance of the teachers or administrators fall below our standards, the parents of those children should recruit more qualified individuals to replace them, and compensate them fairly. All children should be taught computer coding and web-design as core classes, in addition to English, Mathematics, Science and History. This will ensure that every student will be equipped with a trade that he or she can use to find gainful employment at any stage in their life. Thus, if the circumstances of our impoverished children do force them to drop out of school, they may find employment using a lawful skill that is in high demand. Furthermore, the work environment will be a lot more child friendly than a construction site, and thanks to technology, some of these children may even be able to work from home. Thus, the child labor law barrier may be overcome. This in my opinion, is how we must combat the school to prison pipeline. Although this tactic may fall short of completely removing this contaminated structure from America's field of opportunity, it will at least clog up the pipeline enough for us to protect some of our children from being sucked into the system.

P.E.A.C.E.
Please Educate All Children Everywhere

FACT: 100% COLLEGE ACCEPTANCE
URBAN PREP ACADEMIES

URBAN PREP
420 N Wabash, Suite 340 Chicago, IL 60611
First all-male charter high school
Founded 2002 by Tim King

MUHAMMAD UNIVERSITY OF ISLAM

MUHAMMAD UNIVERSITY OF ISLAM
7351 S Stony Island Ave, Chicago, IL 60649

HARLEM PREP MIDDLE SCHOOL

HARLEM PREP MIDDLE SCHOOL
232 E 103rd St, New York, NY 10029
Public Charter School
Founded 2013

TUSKEGEE INSTITUTE
1200 W Montgomery Rd, Tuskegee, AL 36088
Private 4-yr University
Founded 1881 by Booker T. Washington and Lewis Adams

Master's Academy

"Builders Build"

- A school for grades 1-12, with a pre-K option
- All year attendance (40 weeks of school/ 9 weeks of breaks/ 3 week buffers)
- M-F 9hr school day (7am-4pm)? Or 8hr day with ½ day on Sat (9am-1pm)?
- Block scheduling for grades 7-12

CURRICULUM

Language Arts
- Reading and Writing Basics
- English I & English I
- Black Lit Studies
  - Classical
  - Contemporary
- Multicultural Lit
- Comparative Lit
- Debate

- Public Speaking

Social Studies
- U.S. History
- World History
- Black History
  - Classical
  - Diaspora
  - Colonial
  - Contemporary
- Law & Politics
  - Political Theory
  - U.S. Law
  - U.N. Law
- Government Study
- Black Philosophy
  - Classical
  - Contemporary
- Multicultural Philosophy
- Foreign Language
- Civics

Math
- Arithmetic
- Pre-Algebra I & II
- Geometry I & II
- Trigonometry I & II
- Calculus I & II

Self-Awareness

- Power of Thought
- Meditation Techniques
- Elders Study
- You & The World
- Community Service
- Holistic Outlook
- Gender Roles (?)

Phys. Ed.

- Gym
- Health Class
- Eating to Live
- Sex Ed
- Yoga

Art

- Artistic Theory
  - Classical
  - Contemporary
- Art Fundamentals
- Journalism
- Dance
- Film-making
- Computer Graphic Design
- Photography
- Black Music/Music Theory
  - Classical
  - Contemporary
- Black Arts Studies
- Multicultural Music Studies

- Multicultural Art Studies

Science
- Biology
  - General
  - Human
- Astronomy
- Astrology (?)
- Physics
- Botany
- Chemistry
- Geology
- Psychology
- Sociology
- Gen. Science Class
- Engineering

Life Studies
- Business 101
- Economics
- Credit Basics
- Paying Taxes
- Voting
  - Federal
  - State
  - Local
- Money Management
- Home Economics
- Accounting Basics
- Computer Literary/ Typing
- Job Readiness

- ○ Application Process
- ○ Interview & Follow-up
- ○ Workplace Conduct

PROGRAMS & CLUBS

- Gardening/Agriculture
  - ○ Feed the Hungry type program
  - ○ Bartering program
- Fashion Design
  - ○ School Uniform Program
- Vocational Trades (HVAC, Woodshop/Carpentry, Electrical, Plumbing, Masonry, etc.)
  - ○ Habitat for Humanity type of program
  - ○ School Maintenance program
- Band
- Sports
- Tutoring
  - ○ Assistant Teachers/ Teacher-Aide program
- School Paper/Magazine/Website
- Community Outreach Program
- FBLA (Future Business Leaders of America)
  - ○ Candy/Snack Line program
  - ○ Custom clothing program
- School Government
- Environmental Club
- School Spirit Club
  - ○ Dances
  - ○ Parades
  - ○ Pep Rallies
- JROTC-type program

- Self-defense
  - Weapons Training
  - War Strategy
- Art Club
- Music Production
  - School Album

Master's Academy Exposition

When I first devised the idea for the Master's Academy I was just trying to think of some practical solutions to the problems I saw in the black community. This was in 2012, maybe early 2013, and I had just begun to seriously delve into Black liberation thought. One thing that immediately stood out to me was the importance of indoctrination and the way propaganda is used to facilitate this end. I also realized early on that White Supremacy, as an ideology, is upheld and propagated through its institutions and their implicit—sometimes complicit—cooperation. Well, I thought, just as snake venom is used to form an antidote to the poison, so too do our people need to create institutions that can instill a holistic ideology in the minds of the people and utilize the propaganda machine to propagate it. Master's Academy was my first attempt to crystalize the need that I see for institutions of our own—specifically schools.

I envision Master's Academy as an institution that can turn the descendants of American slaves into Masters—masters of themselves, and, by extension, their destinies. The courses that I have included are intended to not only raise our children to the Western standard of excellence but to surpass their ideal and lead the world into a more holistic understanding of Life. Categories like Life Studies and Self-Awareness include courses that take into account the practical mechanistic view of the West while also realizing the transcendental wisdom and metaphysical science of our forefathers—the Masters of Antiquity.

When our ancestors were released from the bonds of chattel slavery they let out a resounding cry for "books!" Those former slaves wanted nothing more than the education that their previous station had denied them and with it the guarantee of a true freedom; for how limited are the choices of the ignorant, how tight their binds? Coming from this desert of learning, where we had wondered the proverbial 40 years and then some, our thirst for knowledge was so great, so pressing, that we took the first cup offered us, unaware that this cup contained the seething mixture of lies and distortion that would lead to Carter G. Woodson's poignantly diagnosed "miseducation." It is this miseducation that must be extirpated if we are to ever achieve the station of Master.

Haile Selassie, Ethiopia's great educational reformer, once said, "Discipline of the mind is a basic ingredient of genuine morality and therefore of spiritual strength. Indeed, a university, taking in all its aspects, is essentially a spiritual enterprise which, along with the knowledge and understanding it imparts, leads students into more wise living and a greater sensitivity to life's responsibilities." This is the aim of the Master's Academy: to make men and women in the truest sense of the word and to place each individual that enters into its walls on a conscious path of self-actualization that will bring more light into the world. Booker T. Washington sought a vocation-centered education for our people while DuBois said we must teach the thinkers to think and the workers to work. I add that the Thinkers must work just as hard as the Workers must think, for in today's world the two are as entwined as life and death. (And maybe this has always been the case.) The Thinkers must not simply think for the sake of thinking, sitting high in their Ivory towers mulling over ideas that have no practical value. Thinkers must think thoughts that will work when brought to the world of form, they must be our problem solvers and innovators, and they must never be afraid to get their own hands dirty; to see themselves as workers for both God and man. The Worker must neither be a brute instrument in the hands of another nor a slave to a consumer lifestyle. Workers must always think of the end that they're working; they must think of better ways to do the work, to make the work easier on those coming behind them; they must think of efficiency in work and life, that more of their time may be devoted to the Great Work, for it is within the workshop of the mind that the greatest labors are performed. The Thinker must think of his brother and the Worker must work for his brother and in doing so their roles become more and more alike; they draw nearer and nearer to each other, until there no longer stand Workers and Thinkers but men and women, kings and queens, gods and goddesses.

In my curriculum, if it can be called such, I have sought to give the students an Afrocentric outlook of the world supplemented with a holistic understanding of other peoples and cultures. In doing this, I expect that there will be those that reject such a curriculum, believing that I am simply trading White Supremacy for Black Supremacy, that no particular cultural reference point is required (i.e., all education should be objective), or that an Afrocentric education is unpatriotic. I will briefly address these points now. First and foremost, diversity rules the phenomenal plane. The physical world consists of a myriad amount things, all differing from each other on the surface but essentially consisting of the same essence. Quantum physics and the Second Law Of Thermodynamics have come to similar conclusions. This being so, diversity is ordained. We cannot run from it. We can only embrace, understand, and utilize it. By teaching African descendants about African views and contributions first, I am only following nature's course. A child is reared in the ways of his family before he or she ventures out to the school and learns about the world beyond their home. Afrocentricity is, as Dr. Molefi Asante explained, "a frame of reference wherein phenomena are viewed from the perspective of the African people... It centers on placing people of African origin in control of their lives and attitudes about the world.

...Afrocentricity is the study of ideas and events from the standpoint of Africans as the key players rather than victims. This theory becomes, by virtue of an authentic relationship to the centrality of our own reality, a fundamentally empirical project...it is Africa asserting itself intellectually and psychologically, breaking the bonds in every other field." Such a study is a necessary treatment for minds suffering from the sickness of White Supremacy and its Black Inferiority counterpart. A person must be properly oriented in time and space if they are to ever have any true sense of direction. To oppose Afrocentricity then, is to desire an inferior state in Black people. And so, to all of my American patriots who feel as if all of us should have the same paradigm (i. e. Eurocentric Western views) I say, America does not treat us all equally; American interests do not always support minority interest; and lastly, America is still a young nation—an aggregation of natives, immigrants, and slaves, giving each of us and ancestral history extending far beyond the borders of this nation. Where is the harm in one remembering and or identifying with their ancestral history?

And although it is Afrocentricity that is taught, I have labeled these courses neither African nor Afro-, but Black. This was done deliberately and for a number of reasons. For one, due to the immigration and theft of her people, the children of Africa are no longer confined to that landmass. The Carribean and the United States (i.e. the Western hemisphere) are home to many descendants who have been long removed from the Motherland and, although they may be separated in locality, culture and nationality, they are united, if by nothing else than by their heavily melaninated skin (i.e. their Black-ness) and the world's response to it. Also, the people of ancient India and Mesopotamia (the Dravidians and Sumerians, respectfully) although not traditionally thought of as members of the African continent, in today's color-coded racial context would be seen as "Black." I also took into account the fact that in 2016, most of Africa's children in America do not refer to themselves as African-American but Black. I also wanted to keep in line with the Black Pride, Black Power, and Black is Beautiful themes of the 20th century.

As a color, black represents the totality of all color while optically it is darkness, the absence of light. But not absence as an ignorance, absence as in the darkness of the womb from which the light was brought forth; that darkness that is the source of all creation. I believe that our ancestral cultures sought to keep this reality in the midst of all learning and it is in the tradition that I have chosen to use the word Black rather than African. Lastly, Africa is not the native name of the landmass but one given to it by foreigners.

In regards to some of the courses and classes that I have included, as stated before, my goal is to raise our students to a higher ideal than the Western World currently promotes. I will give a brief explanation of some of them now. The others should be self-explanatory.

- **Black Literature Studies** seeks to give students an understanding of classical writing styles, themes, and pieces still extant, as well as contemporary styles, themes, and pieces.
- **U.N. Law** is intended to give students an understanding of what the United Nations is, how it functions, why it was created and the laws and orders it has enacted in their application.
- **Governmental Studies** is meant to equip students with an understanding of the various types of governmental institutions that humanity has utilized thus far (their pros, cons, aims, etc.)
- **Black Art Studies** had the same aims as Black Lit Studies but from an artistic perspective not to include music. Its focus will be on drawing, painting, sculpture, and other visual media, as well as artistic philosophy, purposes, themes, etc.
- **Yoga** will teach the importance of Asana yoga, pranayama, and the science of the psycho physical energy centers also known as chakras, as well as their developmental techniques.
- **Eating To Live** teaches healthy dieting, food science, eating habits, etc.

- **The Self-Awareness Category** consists of a series of classes intending to give students an introduction to self actualization.
    - **You And The World** will combine history, sociology, and other disciplines to orient the student in the present day and age.
    - **Gender Roles** will teach healthy meanings of manhood and womanhood based on Afrocentric ideas.
    - **Power Of Thought** teaches will power development, memory enhancement, focus, etc.
    - **Elder's Study** will introduce young children to their ancestors and the contributions that they have made to the human story.
    - **Community Service** introduces students to active community membership and gets them involved and helping others.
    - **Holistic Outlook** will focus on the interdependence of life and how the parts work together to bring about a fully functioning whole (in relation to mind, body, spirit, community, environment, art, [sounds and images], nation and global relations.)
- **The Life Studies Category** consists of a set of courses seeking to endow students with practical skills and knowledge of how to function as an adult in the Western world. It seeks to make each individual self-sufficient as a person.

Master's Academy is intended to be a primary and secondary institution that one enters as a child of 3 to 4 years old and exits at 17 to 18 years old. The categories and courses are intended to be spread out over the duration of a student's education, increasing in complexity, nuance and applicability as the student progresses. Whether traditional grading scales will be utilized is a question that I will leave to those with more knowledge than I. Rites of passage rituals can also be employed to make transitioning between wings a transformational experience.

As concerns the setting, the Academy is envisioned as one large campus with individual wings for the elementary, middle, and high school students; a shared dining area, gym facility, library, auditorium and common area; as well as other various shared spaces.

The academy is thought to be administered by a board of Principals, each serving over their respective wing, who come together to make decisions that affect the entire school body, while retaining autonomy in their own wing. These Principals will work with the various department heads beneath them in order to make sound and well-informed decisions, and these department heads will work with the teachers under them, so that responsibility and power is shared by all and promotion is merit-based.

The faculty is imagined as being very hands-on and able to communicate well with each other and the students. Class sizes are not to exceed 15 students per teacher, except in cases where a large class size better facilitates learning and/or participation or, at the very least, it does not hinder it. I believe that having such a hands-on staff will engender a sense of familiarity between students and staff that will transfer over to a level of accountability and openness. It is hard for a 16 year old to be tough and pretentious in his class when he or she continues to see the same elementary teacher that remembers when he wet himself. And, ideally, the older students will be able to function as role models and mentors for their younger counterparts, keeping down negative behaviors like bullying and hazing.

Master's Academy is attending to, along with the spiritual/religious institution, function as a hub for the community that everyone supports and contributes to. Night school can be offered for adults seeking more training, and community meetings, parent-teacher conferences, etc, should be held regularly. The entire village must be invested in raising its children.

The programs and clubs that I have listed are intended to give the students a practical experience of the knowledge they gained in class and a place to explore their talents and interests, while simultaneously teaching them morals like teamwork, collective responsibility, creativity, unity, self-determination, cooperative economics, faith and purpose. The programs also seek to give the students an investment in the institution by making them responsible (along with staff and faculty) for aspects of the Academy's day-to-day operation. Things like the snack line, school uniforms, school dances, pep rallies, fundraisers, and school government will be under the students' control. For example, the Fashion Design students will design and manufacture the school uniforms that the School Spirit students must approve, that the FBLA students will sell, in accords with the policy enacted and enforced by the School Government, who works with the school administration. I believe that such an educational institution will display the manner in which a society functions, instilling the fundamental principles of nation building in our children's minds, an essential education if our people are to continue to grow towards liberty. Master's Academy, as it is now, it's not a finished idea. I have thought of other questions, programs, and clubs since its 2013 inception, and I am sure that there are far greater minds than mine that are able to take this idea further than I could ever imagine. Master's Academy is my small attempt to develop a theory that can be put into action. The task of bringing this idea to the realm of form will not be an easy one. A suitable location must be found and secured, staff and faculty retained, equipment purchased, accreditation gained, relationships developed, money raised, and most importantly, our people must be made to believe in the idea to the point that they will trust us with the education of their children. This is by far the most important factor, for if the people can be duly convinced, necessity its self will provide us with the solution to any problems that may arise. Or so I hope.

—September 21, 2016
Saint Sincere Quintessence Allah (Q. Jones III) 120°+

CONFEDERATE IMAGERY AND BLACK RESISTANCE

On August 12, 2017 the "Unite the Right Rally" was held in Charlottesville, Virginia. This protest was organized by David Duke, Grand Wizard of the Ku Klux Klan and other White nationalist organizations who were protesting the removal of civil war monuments. This particular monument was a statue of the Confederate General Robert E. Lee. However, this protest erupted into a race riot that left one woman dead.

When questioned by the press about his thoughts on the Charlottesville race riot, President Trump responded by stating there were good people on both sides. This statement received universal rebuke and condemnation from both Democrats and Republicans alike. Both of whom publicly challenged the President to condemn White nationalism, but he would not. Instead President Trump would double down and justify his statement by praising Robert E. Lee as a great general, and he even seemed to oppose the idea of states removing these Civil War monuments due to their support of slavery. President Trump believes that if this prevailed, it would eventually lead to other monuments, such as President Lincoln or even statues of George Washington being removed as well, because, these historical figures either held slaves or supported the institution of slavery.

It has become clear to me that one of the Achilles's heels of Black revolution here in America is our people's short sightedness. Our lack of success in achieving changes with long term sustainability is due partly to our proneness to be misdirected by superficiality. What I am about to say will be unpopular to a lot of people, but it is the truth. From a logical standpoint, President Trump is correct. If Black resistance is successful in removing all the Confederate statues, this should naturally lead to the removal of every statue of any historical figure who has a racist background. But this would be foolish in my opinion. The statue is a symbol of hate, this is true. But the statue also represents a reality Blacks seem to be unwilling to face. And that is, that America has always been racist. Do you think just because White people protest with you and also seek to have these statues removed this makes that history any less true? The fact that the White liberal supports the idea of removing these statues should automatically raise your antennas.

What effect will removing those statues have on this nation in the long term? Do you believe that with each statue removed this will somehow result in one less racist White person? Do you think the removal of these statues will prevent these racists Whites from teaching their children to hate Blacks? Do you think the removal of these statues can protect young Black men from being killed by police? Will it do anything to increase Black earning power? What about the quality of our kids education? Does the removal of Confederate statues improve it or will the removal of these statues make a further contribution to the miseducation of Black youth? In my opinion, these statues are not just a form of outdated art. These statues represent a historical period; these statues are time capsules. These Confederate statues are the imagery of America's ugly past and anyone who supports the removal of them, supports the idea of concealing the truth. Those who wish to conceal this truth from Black youth are attempting to handicap them and set them up for failure. By supporting the removal of Confederate statues you, whether Black or White, are supporting an idea that is a lie, and that is the lie that racism does not exist.

If you really want to challenge the idea being propagated by this Confederate imagery then **PLEASE DO NOT** fight to remove any statues, instead, you **MUST** fight to erect new statues that represent Black resistance to slavery. Tell Mayor Levar Stoney of Richmond, Virginia not to remove any of those Confederate statues on

Monument Avenue. Black activist, please push Mayor Stoney to get the city of Richmond to **erect new statues of Gabriel Prosser and Nat Turner in that same square**. Tell these mayors, if they really wish to support Black resistance to Confederate imagery (or images of White oppression) then do not try to misdirect us with superficial controversy. Do not try to rewrite history by pretending these things didn't happen. No, we want you to tell both sides of the story, and this can only be done by erecting new monuments and statues right next to the Confederate ones. Furthermore, we want these statues designed and made exclusively by Black artists and sculptors.

President Trump is not only a member of the White elite but he is also openly racist. This is why he opposes the removal of these statues. I fully understand why people like David Duke and Trump oppose the removal of these Confederate statues, because it represents the suppression of their ideals and values. Thus, it is no secret what their agenda is. But what is the agenda of the White liberal? Are they really our

Charlottesville, VA "Unite the Right" Rally

ally? I think Blacks have begun to realize that the true agenda of the White liberal is to impede Black progress by misdirecting us and instigating superficial battles, or redefining our struggle in a way that makes it ineffective. Too often Blacks celebrated the superficial images of the White liberal, treating them as our idols of salvation, when really these are the Trojan horses of White oppression, and the key to their infiltration.

Take for instance the images of Bill Clinton playing his saxophone, smoking weed and cheating on his wife. These images gained him universal acceptance as our first Black president, and as a result we dropped our guard and got sucker punched with a crime bill that would nurture the embryo of the 13th Amendment. It was the Clinton Crime Bill that gave birth to mass

President Lyndon B. Johnson handing Civil Rights Leader Martin Luther King Jr. the pen he used to sign the Civil Rights Act of 1964

incarceration. True, Hillary Clinton would pay for it in 2016 and lose the support of many millennial Blacks when past statements calling Black youth "super predators" came back to haunt her. This indicates that Black people are beginning to wake up, and have become wiser in our dealings with White liberals. However, we are not fully woke yet if we allow the fight to remove Confederate statues to be commandeered by the White liberal agenda. Therefore, I write these words to caution the Black activist on their vulnerability, and warn them about how they can be infiltrated by White liberals, who wish to use the fight to remove Confederate images to distract us or misdirect us away from attacking the substance of the problem.

Yes, those Confederate leaders were racist, but so were many of the members of the Union, including Abraham Lincoln, who went on record and stated if he could have saved the Union without freeing the slaves he would have done so. Black people cannot afford to allow the White liberal to use the Confederate image ban

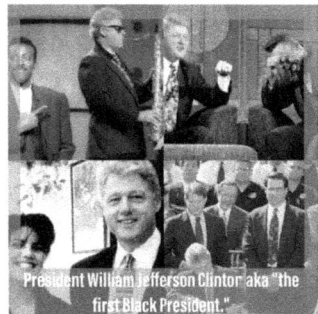

President William Jefferson Clinton aka "the first Black President."

as his Easy Pass back into our hearts. It is not the image or form of things that oppresses Blacks, it is their substance. Those statues are only images, White hatred is the substance from which these images derive. The Confederate statues are just one of many different images or forms, that have manifested from the substance of White hatred of Blacks. If Blacks should fight for the removal of one racist statue then it is only logical that we fight for the removal of all racist statues. For Blacks to be offended at Confederate statues or even the Confederate flag, but to embrace statues of the founding fathers or the American flag is hypocritical. **I challenge you to name one abuse Blacks have been subjected to under the Confederate flag that our people have not suffered under the authority of the American one.**

The Confederacy is an undeniable part of American history but so is slavery. We do not support revisionist history, and we will not pretend that these things didn't happen. Until the White liberal begins tearing down the White power structure, this new symbolic gesture of tearing down Confederate statues, is just another red herring. The real problem in America is that, with the exception of John Brown and a handful of others, there have been very few Whites who have been willing to perform this symbolic gesture, because this image can only be shown by Whites who possess a substantial amount of love for the Black race as their fellow citizens, but more importantly, as a fellow member of humanity. The sincere White liberal who wishes to aid us in tearing down the White power structure, will zealously fight to remove the statutes that oppress Black people who live today, but the one whose focus is limited to statues that

oppressed Black people who are now all dead, is not fighting against the White power structure, they are fighting to gain more power within it. The integrationists of our generation must gain the wisdom to discern the difference between the two. Peace!

"TRUMPet"

By Lord Serious

Winds, percussions, brass, and strings,
who in America made the TRUMPet king?
Open the symphony with chimes and snares,
out of nowhere the TRUMPet blares
With no maestro to conduct the score,
a harmonic orchestra becomes no more
Those who fell victim to the TRUMPet's ploy,
are killing music by making noise
The dissonance of this staged event,
sounds like unrest and discontent
A tyranny begins when free press ends,
the whistleblower is silent without winds
TRUMPet's solo became a grave discussion,
M.A.G.A by hating African percussions
The Spanish guitar was viewed as regal,
until the TRUMPet called the strings illegal
The TRUMPet was a part of an elitist class,
the rich and affluent American brass
While the TRUMPet claimed every note it blew,
was an octave of red, white and blue
The 45th symphony showed the TRUMPet was a,
instrument in our orchestra owned by Russia

- Bravo! TRUMPet, bravo!
you have stolen the show, bravo!
A bandit and a thief, bravo!
you're killing democracy, bravo!

APOTHEOSIS AND THE FOUNDING OF THE KINGDOM OF GOD RIGHT HERE ON EARTH

"As we know, whenever there is a longing or demand for a change, nature will produce that man, who will bring it about."
- The Honorable Elijah Muhammad

For those who are in the know, the signs of the times are very revealing. One of the most allegorical books in the Bible is the Book of Revelations. Many people believe that no one truly knows what the real interpretation of this book is. The Bible, like the Holy Qur'an are both history books written by the Original man. The history of our people's past, present and future are all contained within the contents of their parchment pages. I am not a religious man, so I am not here to promote any particular religion. I am here to teach you the culture of our ancestors and to inform you of the truth that these books contain. It is a truth that will empower the Black, Brown, and Yellow people in America. Therefore, it is a truth that the White power structure wishes to keep concealed. Within this appeal I have made many accurate predictions. But I have not come to make prophecy. I have come to teach future generations what they must do to fulfill prophecy.

My understanding of what has taken place in the past gives me insight on what's yet to come. There's nothing supernatural about this, it's just cause and effect. It was through utilizing this same mental ability that our ancestors showed their supreme understanding of sociology and psychology and made predictions about what they expected to come to pass, and then they recorded these predictions so that future progeny would have them to use at their disposal when the time was right. I cannot speak for how the religious man understands these things, so if you want that breakdown you should ask your clergyman. But from a cultural standpoint we have always held a high level of respect for the wisdom of our ancestors. So the fact that many of us believe that these books and the men who wrote them hold supernatural powers isn't really all that surprising.

But I find myself questioning what kind of God would give us intelligence then give us a book to instruct us on how to worship him and live a righteous life, but then make it too complex for any of us to understand? Being literate means you possess the ability to read and write. Well, reading consists of more than just being able to phonetically recite letters or pronounce words. To read you must be able to comprehend what is written and interpret what the author means. And if you cannot do this sufficiently, then you will most likely lack the ability to know how to take your place in history by observing these patterns of behavior and then putting yourself in a position where you can take advantage of future opportunities. This is how you write your own history in advance. Whether you believe the God who wrote these books is an invisible being who cannot be seen by the physical eye, or if you're like me, and you see God and the Black men who wrote these books as being one and the same; this chapter will instruct you on how you can contribute to the fulfillment of prophecy.

THE FOUR HORSEMEN

"Now I saw when the Lamb opened one of the seals; and I heard one of the four living creatures saying with a voice like thunder, "Come and see." And I looked, and behold, a white horse. He who sat on it had a bow; and a crown was given to him, and he went out conquering and to conquer." - Revelations 6:1-2

The opening of the first seal reveals the rider of the white horse as being a hero ready for battle.

"When He opened the second seal, I heard the second living creature saying, "Come and see." Another horse, fiery red, went out. And it was granted to the one who sat on it to take peace from the earth, and that people should kill one another; and there was given to him a great sword." - Revelations 6:3-4

The second seal reveals the red horseman whose rider takes peace away from the people of the Earth by causing war.

"When He opened the third seal, I heard the third living creature say, "Come and see." So I looked, and behold, a black horse, and he who sat on it had a pair of scales in his hand. And I heard a voice in the midst of the four living creatures saying, "A quart of wheat for a denarius, and three quarts of barley for a denarius; and do not harm the oil and the wine." - Revelations 6:5-6

Now the third seal reveals a black horseman who seems to be selling/buying goods and trading commodities; and lastly:

"When He opened the fourth seal, I heard the voice of the fourth living creature saying, "Come and see." So I looked, and behold, a pale horse. And the name of him who sat on it was Death, and Hades followed him. And power was given to them over a fourth of the earth, to kill with sword, with hunger, with death, and by the beasts of the earth." - Revelations 6:7-8

The fourth seal not only reveals a pale horseman, but it also tells us the rider's name is Death and Hell (or Hades) follows him. Now what if I told you that the four horsemen of revelations are not an evil supernatural force that has yet to come? What if I told you these four horsemen are four historical events that describe a specific group of people in a specific location? Have you figured it out yet? If you guessed the location was the U.S.A and the people are the White race then you are correct. When the White race left Europe to colonize the new world they did it in the name of their kings and queens (or wearing a crown on their head), carrying a rifle (or a bow with invisible arrows), on a mission to conquer. Some even called themselves conquistadors which is Spanish and translates as conquering/conquer. So after leaving Europe as heroes they reach the wilderness of North America and began waging a savage war against the peace loving Native Americans whom they disparagingly called the Red man. The third Horseman rides the Black horse and he seems to be preoccupied with commerce. Ironically, all of the commodities listed in that verse: wheat, barley, oil and wine were all staples of the Trans-Atlantic slave trade of the Black man, woman and child. Finally, the fourth horseman reveals to the world that the White race is a race that brings Death to the Original people everywhere they go, and the moment they show up on your land Hell soon follows. If there is 29 million square miles of useful land on the

75

planet earth and the White race uses 6 million square miles, then they have been given power to subdue between 1/4th - 1/5th of the Earth with their sword. The truth has always been simple. Lies are complex and complicated.

But as mind blowing as this is, Revelations contains so much more. It actually instructs us on what we must do to overcome the oppression of White supremacy. We must establish the kingdom of God right here on Earth.

THE KINGDOM OF GOD

"...the kingdom of God does not come with observation; nor will they say, 'See here!' or 'See there!' For indeed, the kingdom of God is within you." - Luke 17:20-21

Jesus taught that the kingdom of heaven was not up in the sky, but it was within you. For so long we have been taught by our enslavers that we should continue to go through hell on Earth suffering peaceably, because by remaining obedient and meek we would inherit our heaven in the afterlife. They continue daily to teach this interpretation of the word of God, and this is believed by many of you. But our enslavers know that when a man dies he will never return to tell the living whether he lied or not. But while Black people have been going through hell the White race have been enjoying their heaven on Earth at our expense.

"Now I saw a new heaven and a new earth, for the first heaven and the first earth had passed away..." - Revelations 21:1

This prophecy informs us that a change is coming. Those who enjoyed the first heaven and the first earth, their time is running short and a new heaven and earth shall soon be established.

"Then I, John, saw the holy city, New Jerusalem, coming down out of heaven from God, prepared as a bride adorned for her husband." - Revelations 21:2

It was the custom of the ancient world to place the temple of God in the center of the city so that all of its inhabitants would be an equal distance away from God. Jerusalem is the name given by the Jews and means "Founded in peace". However, the city was first built by the Original people and was called Jebus, Salem and Ariel. Modern day Jerusalem is located in Palestine, which is in Asia minor. However, the New Jerusalem will be founded in the center of that city's namesake Jer-USA-lem. Translation - The United States Of America.

"He who overcomes shall inherit all things, and I will be his God and he shall be My son." - Revelations 21:7

One of the Ten Commandments instructs us that we have a duty to honor our father and mother so that our days shall be longer upon the earth. If we lived our lives in accordance with our ancestors' natural way of life we would overcome the adversities and challenges that come from our futile attempt to assimilate into this western culture. By adhering to the culture of our forefathers we could join the pantheon of Black visionaries and statesmen who founded civilizations long before the White race came into existence. If we would reclaim our own culture, we would carry on the ancient African tradition of taking on the name of God and make our ancestral lineage known.

"But the cowardly, unbelieving, abominable, murderers, sexually immoral, sorcerers, idolaters, and all liars shall have their part in the lake which burns with fire and brimstone, which is the second death." - Revelations 21:8

What this verse is alluding to is what will happen to all those who choose to do otherwise. If you fear the wrath of the White race for daring to be man enough to want better for your people then you are a coward. If you do not believe the wisdom of our ancestors is right and exact then you are an unbeliever. If you would rather live an unrighteous lifestyle by doing any of the remaining acts or deeds then you will be apprehended and punished by being inflicted with the second death. In case you didn't know, the mental death is the first death inflicted upon us while we were babies. Western civilization indoctrinates Black children to grow up having an inferiority complex and this subconscious handicap can only be overcome by gaining knowledge of self. The second death you will suffer is not a physical death, it is a civil death. You will be sent to a prison/jail where you will have little to no rights. The third death is a physical death. I am not physically dead, but I was once mentally dead. I am now currently striving to recover from a civil death.

THE NATION OF GODS AND EARTHS

In case you didn't know, I am a member of the Nation of Gods and Earths. However, no one member is authorized to speak for our entire nation. Like other nations we are also a diverse group of people. We do not all think the same or view life through the same lens. The Nation of Gods and Earths has no leaders or followers, but we are all taught to be leaders within our communities. With that said I will now further enlighten the world on the significance of our nation, and my understanding of the purpose for which it was founded.

"Behold, I send My messenger, And he will prepare the way before Me. And the Lord, whom you seek, Will suddenly come to His temple, Even the Messenger of the covenant, In whom you delight. Behold, He is coming," Says the Lord of host."
-Malachi 3:1

A man by the name of Clarence Smith received an honorable discharge from the U.S. Army after fighting in the Korean War from 1952-1960. In 1960 he returned home to his wife and kids in Harlem, New York, where he would be introduced to the teachings of the Honorable Elijah Muhammad, the Messenger of God and the leader of the Nation of Islam. After visiting Temple #7 and listening to the passionate address of Minister Malcolm X, this man decided to join the Nation of Islam. Because he was the 13th Clarence to join this temple he would receive the surname 13X. Clarence 13X stayed in the Temple with the Messenger for about three years before coming into the realization that he was the Black God that the Muslim lessons spoke about. The Book of Malachi had prophesied these events over 2,500 years in advance, and this was indeed prophecy fulfilled.

The Muslim lessons were brought to the wilderness of North America by the Prophet W.F Muhammad. The Detroit history states that Prophet W. F. Muhammad first came to the U.S. in 1910 to study the conditions of the Black race. It states he left and came back again in 1914, which he prophesied would be the expiration date of White Supremacy. But the Prophet W.F Muhammad realized that not enough Black people in the U.S. had gained knowledge of self yet, so a 50 year grace period was given to the White race. Now when you add 50 years to the year 1914 you arrive at the year 1964. There was a lot of political unrest in the U.S. over segregation and the Civil Rights Movement at this time. Although much of the attention was focused on the elder Civil Rights leaders, the youth played a prominent role in fighting for change too. After leaving Temple #7 in 1963, Clarence 13X was no more. He was now Allah and he had a plan to save the world through the children. 1964 would mark Year One and the founding of the Nation of Gods and Earths.

After Malcolm X's death the Counter Intelligence Program (COINTELPRO) under the guidance of FBI Director J. Edgar Hoover put out a memorandum that their mission was to stop the rise of the next Black Messiah. They acknowledged that had Malcolm still been alive he would be the most likely candidate. Coincidentally, the first youth taught by Allah was named Black Messiah. Although Black Messiah was the first to receive the knowledge from Allah and we honor him as such, every Black man who comes into the consciousness of knowing that they are God and then chooses to live a righteous life by teaching Freedom, Justice, and Equality to all human families of the planet Earth has become the next Black Messiah. Anyone who opposes this is being an Anti-Christ. Christ is not Jesus' last name. Christ is a title like King, Guru, or Buddha. There have been numerous Christs throughout history and the word derives from the Greek *kristos* which means "anointed one" or Messiah. Therefore, the Nation of Gods and Earths is a nation full of Black Messiahs, and because we have no central leadership, killing any one particular member would be senseless, because as long as we continue teaching Allah cannot die!

In my humble opinion, the Nation of Gods and Earths has continued to play a pivotal role in the fulfillment of prophecy since its inception. I will show and prove without going too deep. I do not want to talk over people's heads so I will give you enough information to permit all those who wish to know more to do their own independent research and further their understanding on the matter at hand. Although Allah left the Temple, the Messenger had indeed prepared the way for him with the Muslim lessons. Allah gave a redacted version of these teachings to the youth and instructed them to study their lessons and to use the Supreme Mathematics and Supreme Alphabets as the keys to unlock their hidden meaning. These Eight Point Lessons which are represented by the Eight Points of my nation's Universal flag have opened my mind to understanding life on a deeper level. I do not look at the Bible as something mystical, nor do I believe every passage is literal. Much of it is allegorical, and most people lack the ability to unlock the hidden meaning simply because they are trying to interpret it through the culture of the people whom the book is about and not through the culture of those who wrote it.

The Bible is about the White race. Jewish and Christian scholars agree that the Book of Genesis begins about 6,000 years ago. This time frame does not coincide with scientific evidence for how long the Universe has been in existence. But it does coincide with scientific evidence proving how long the White race has been in existence. The Book of Genesis is an allegorical story that records the beginning of the White race, not the beginning of the Universe. The same Original people who wrote your beloved Bible also predicted the emergence of the White race long before any of these events took place. You have been fooled into believing that climate is the only factor for their different skin color. But Black people have inhabited cold high altitude climates for years. Why haven't the Tibetan monks of the Himalayas lost their skin pigmentation or the Inuits who live in the arctic region of North America? It doesn't get much colder than that. Yet these Brown people are still Brown. So how did these people develop their pale White skin? And why does the psychology of White Supremacy keep them at odds with nature and the Original inhabitants of the planet earth? These answers are all revealed within the Bible.

As I stated before I am not anti-white nor am I pro-black. I do not hate the White race. I understand them and it is this understanding that leads me to warn the world what they have in store for the Original people. Every White person is not out to get us. But there are enough of them in positions of power who are. The John Browns of the world should be given a righteous embrace. But far too many times we have been fooled by the Clintons of the world. So we should not trust any of them. It is time that we learn to do for self, and if they really love Black people they will respect our desire to exercise self determination as a race of people. Nevertheless, the White power structure does everything in its power to undermine the progress of the Black and Brown people who call the U.S. their home.

Let me enlighten you on a few basic facts about where this country is headed, then maybe you will better understand why they treat people who look like me as their enemy. It has been projected that by 2050 the White population in the U.S. will no longer be the majority. It is because they fear being mistreated by us, should we take political power away from them, that they employ every dirty trick known to man to oppress and repress us as a people. The birth/death ratio of the White race is deficient. White women are not giving birth to the 2.5 children needed to maintain stable population growth. This means that, without any intervention, a time will come when the White race will no longer exist. This is not me being a racist, people, I am just highlighting the facts.

With this new information we can now better understand their pathological behavior, hostile mistreatment and abuse of the Original people. If I was a member of a race who had such a wicked history of mistreating another race, I too would be worried about retaliation should those people become the political majority. To prevent this from happening or to hinder it from happening, some White people seem to believe it is in their race's best interest to use their political power to frustrate the progression of Blacks. They accomplish this by pushing "get tough on crime" legislation with mandatory minimums and use the law to criminalize the behavior of those they fear; the resulting mass incarceration of Black and Brown men was a logical and desired effect of these policies. The psychology of the White Supremacist thinks that it is logical to pass immigrant legislation banning people from "shit hole countries" from entering the U.S. Within the White Supremacist psyche it has now become logical to reinterpret current immigration policy in a manner that authorizes them to separate immigrant children from their parents and keep them confined inside cages and unsanitary living conditions. What will these poor displaced children grow to become if such abuse is permitted to continue unabated? It is the psychology of White supremacy that creates enemies out of peace loving Black, Brown and Yellow people everywhere. America I am warning you, do not force these children to grow up despising you and all you stand for.

Because they too will produce one from amongst themselves who will make you regret your mistreatment of their people.

Black and Brown people can choose to be divided and feel like we don't have any skin in the game when it comes to the others struggle. But I feel the need to remind you both of what American history teaches us. The White power structure is willing to do anything to check our population growth and once the Brown people on the southern border have been subdued there is no one left to stop them from committing their worst sins against Blacks. It was after killing and taking the land from the ancestors of today's Brown people that the White race could then focus all of their aggression on the Black race without interference. So if these people feel emboldened enough to cage foreign nationals and separate parents from their children without fear of repercussion from the governments of Mexico and other Central American countries, just think what they will have in store for a nationless race of Black people with no government to protect them?

In addition to this, after being informed that their race is dying out, the more powerful members amongst them felt they had a moral obligation to do something to extend their time here on the planet. For those with the power to do so, it was logical to pass legislation banning abortion. As I stated earlier, the U.S. is a White male dominated society and even some homosexual White men want White babies. However, White babies can only be produced by White women. So whether their women likes it or not, no woman will be permitted to abort their pregnancy, regardless of rape or incest in states where these men hold power.

But if you think that's extremely selfish of them, allow me to explain how the imbalance in their race's birth to mortality ratio leads the psychology of White supremacy to reject the real danger of climate change. For some of these White men in power it appears that their rationale for rejecting and denying the scientific community's findings is partly financial, but it is also deeply rooted in their understanding that their race's time here on Earth is limited. Since they will not be able to enjoy the planet for much longer their selfishness and hatred leads them to pass legislation that repealed carbon emission safety standards and government regulation. Then to discourage others from being more Earth friendly "Bankrupt Trump" sues the state of California for requiring car companies to do more to lower CO_2 output in their vehicle's exhausts.

HOW MUCH MORE TIME DOES WHITE SUPREMACY HAVE TO RULE?

I'm not sure how many of you are into astronomy or astrology. But I will try to keep things simple. What we know as time is really the measurement of movement. Nowadays most of us depend on man-made clocks to keep track of time. But the original clock used by the Original people of the planet Earth was and is, the Sun, Moon, and Stars. Our ancestors measured the movements of the heavenly bodies to keep track of the days, months, seasons, years, and cyclel ages. But when it comes to measuring shorter periods of time like seconds, minutes and hours a watch is much more convenient. However, I began this book by explaining that our people's struggle was a protracted one, which means something that is long or it's a drawn out process. The wise Black men who wrote the Bible, and those who predicted the birth of the White race also predicted the destruction of White supremacy. The Prophet W. F. Muhammad taught the Messenger Elijah Muhammad that the expiration of Western Civilization was 1914 which was the year World War I began. But a grace period had to be given, because not enough Black people had gained knowledge of self yet. This grace period would last 50 years and takes us to 1964 or Year One of the Nation of Gods and Earths. The year that Allah taught Black youth in the streets of Harlem the knowledge of self. He then instructed these youth to teach 10 people younger than themselves and to teach those they taught to do the same. But as it concerns keeping track of the time within this cycle age 1964 is an extremely important year.

To understand this you must have an understanding of the Earth's movements. Although when we look up in the sky it appears as though the Sun, Moon and Stars are moving around the Earth, we know that the Earth is actually rotating on its axis. We also know in addition to this movement that the Earth also revolves around the Sun. It takes the Earth approximately 24 hours to complete its rotation on its axis and 360 days to revolve around the Sun. The 5.25 days are added because it takes the stars that long to catch up. The first movement is how we measure our days and the second is how we measure years. However, the Earth is tilted on its axis and this tilt is what permits most of the planet to experience four seasons. Due to this tilt, the Sun passes over the Earth's equator and warms the northern hemisphere in the summer and passes below the equator during our winter. The tilt of the Earth and its unique wobble causes its axis to trace a path through the entire zodiac belt. This is called the precision of the Earth's axis and it takes approximately 25,000 years to complete. This 25,000 year period marks the completion or expiration of the heavenly (Holy) Qur'an. The zodiac belt is a region in space where 12 constellations align. These constellations (or signs) aided humanity in keeping track of the seasons and permitted us to develop the 12 month calendar. Each zodiac sign has a house or zone so massive that it takes the Earth's axis 2,160 years to move from one house to the next. This movement and its 2,160 year period make up a cycle age. The zodiac belt is a Universal clock. Like the face of an analog clock this Universal clock is also divided into 12 sections. Each section has 30 degrees. However, on the Universal clock each one of these 30 degrees last for a period of 72 years. The year 1964 marks the beginning of the 30th degree in what most people consider the cycle age of Pisces. If you add 72 years to 1964 you will arrive at the year

2036. This will mark the beginning of the Aquarian age (night sign). But really it will be the age of Leo (day sign).This has major implications with understanding the Book of Revelations. Here's why:

THE 24 SCIENTISTS

"Around the throne were twenty-four thrones, and on the thrones I saw twenty-four elders sitting, clothed in white robes; and they had crowns of gold on their heads." - Revelations 4:4

These 24 thrones with elders sitting on them represent the 12 houses or zones on the zodiac belt and the 12 constellations (or zodiac signs) which make a total of 24 elders sitting on thrones.

THE FOUR CREATURES

"Before the throne there was a sea of glass, like crystal. And in the midst of the throne, and around the throne, were four creatures full of eyes in front and in back. The first living creature was like a lion, the second living creature like a calf, the third living creature had a face like a man, and the fourth living creature was like a flying eagle." -Revelations 4:6-7

The four creatures are full of eyes front and back because they are constellations full of stars. The first constellation is like a lion and represents the zodiac sign Leo. The second creature is like a calf and represents the zodiac sign Taurus. The fourth creature had a face like a man and represents the zodiac sign Aquarius. The fourth creature is like that of a flying eagle, though none of the zodiac signs are eagles this creature represents Scorpio. However, the flying eagle is the insignia of the U.S. government and it can be found on everything from official government letterheads to U.S. currency. The positioning of these signs on the zodiac belt shows that Leo is directly across from Aquarius and Taurus is directly across from Scorpio. In astrology this arrangement is called a "Fixed Cross" or the "Cross of Soul".

This gives us a more accurate indication on when we should expect the final reckoning of the Book of Revelations to be fulfilled. The destruction of Western civilization will happen in One Day which is a thousand years to God. So the approximate time frame for the destruction of White Supremacy and all of its adverse effects is around 2964. This is the latest it could happen, but we have the power to speed the process up if we so choose. We must continue to teach and raise the conscious of the people. When the collective consciousness of the Original people has reached a critical mass we will no longer be so divided. We will unite in righteousness and their reign will be over.

The Book of Revelations calls this the battle of Armageddon. Many of you believe the story about this battle is literal so you are expecting something supernatural to occur. But little do you know we are fighting that battle right now as we speak. There will be those amongst us who will claim what I'm suggesting cannot be done. But do not allow this to discourage you. Remember, old ideas do not die, until old people do. It is this type of defeatist subservient thinking that constrains our ability to liberate ourselves. It is this inferiority complex with its crippling fear that relegates us to a life of servitude and dependency within their system. You must teach to rid our people of this way of thinking or it may take a thousand years for them to forget it on their own.

However, there is no guarantee that the White race will survive that long. They could all perish like other homo sapiens species have done in the past. In fact, Elijah Muhammad stated that they would not live to see the year 7,000. So that gives them until 2914 before they become extinct. Yet, the Blacks who remain could still be negatively affected by their culture long after they've disappeared. So the way I interpret the prophecy is that this is the length of time it will take the Original people to recover and begin living life as we did before slavery and colonization. I am not saying we will revert back to the days of using smoke signals because we don't have the internet. I'm saying we will once again adhere to a way of life that keeps us in peace and harmony with each other and our environment.

It has not been revealed to me what the lifespan of the U.S. government will be. Allah stated that the White race would not trust us with running the government until we were righteous. He also taught that we should respect the government and if they did right by us we should fight to preserve it. I respect all governments even hostile ones. And in my judgment the U.S. government has not been doing right by us. However, Allah also warned the government that if they didn't do right by us then eventually one of his 5%ers would deal with them a lot more harshly than he did. He told government officials that many of his 5%ers had been locked up in institutions and many of us were bitter about it. Personally I think I feel more righteous indignation than bitterness towards this government. But in either case, this doesn't mean that I'm wrong in my assessment of things. It just means that my dissatisfaction with them has reached a level where I will give all that I have and all within my power to live to see the day which I have waited for 464 years to the date of this writing.

As much as I dislike the way this government is being run, I am not encouraging anarchy or a revolt against it. However, I did not appreciate Bankrupt Trump's call for those Black and Brown Congresswomen to "Go back where they came from." That type of behavior is unacceptable and I wouldn't care if he was a White beggar or the POTUS. Before any racist White person opens their mouth like that again, they should keep in mind that the entire Earth belongs to the Original people and this has been our home long before your ancestors found shelter in the caves of the Caucasus mountains. So do not continue to disrespect our women in our home, because you are the one who is the guest, not us. We don't have to go anywhere, and the fact that these kinds of comments can be said by the President of this country to minority women who are legislatures is troubling and indicative that the path to a better America is not the one way street of integration as many of you believe. There is a core group of White Americans who will always be resistant to this change and the increase in mass shootings proves that these core beliefs are something they are prepared to kill and die for. We are living in a dangerous time here in America. But we have overcome worse. The problem is that America was a much younger country back then; it was still trying to find its identity. I think the U.S. we live in today is a very self aware country. It knows who it is, and what it will live to become. As well as knowing who it is not, and what it will never become. And though America reminds us of this every chance it gets, Blacks still refuse to believe it.

Therefore any policy or program being pushed by us moving forward cannot be strictly an integrationist one. If it is then it is not a policy designed to move us forward. It is one designed to reveal our insanity (doing the same thing over and over again but expecting different results). Without Blacks and immigrants this country would not be as strong as it is. Yet, we have continuously been underappreciated. So we should do all we can to preserve and advance our political power within the U.S. government as a short term goal. But our long term goal should be to secure our own nationhood separate and independent from the U.S. government.

Here's how we begin:

LAYING THE FOUNDATION

We must be able to feed ourselves. The long term effects of climate change will cause more extreme weather. You should expect more severe hurricanes, tornadoes, flooding, mud slides, wildfires and earthquakes. These conditions will eventually affect growing seasons adversely, causing food shortages, famine, sickness and death for those who are ill prepared. I recommend that we begin growing communal gardens. If you live in government housing, petition those on your city council for approval to use a vacant city lot or receive a land designation. We should grow natural alkaline vegetables and herbs. Dr. Sebi has made it known which vegetables and herbs are best to heal and nourish our gene type. The herbs should be used to heal the sick and elderly who cannot afford to pay high prices for hospital visits and prescription drugs. The vegetables should be prepared and consumed as a communal meal where every inhabitant of that community is welcome as long as they come in peace. If you could get enough neighboring communities to do the same it should produce a sufficient enough yield to begin phase two.

The goal at this juncture is for the community to produce enough food that it is able to feed itself every night. When we master that our next phase is to produce enough of a surplus that it can be sold to a foreign government. After we learn to feed ourselves we have a responsibility to help feed our Black and Brown brothers and sisters abroad. The goal here is to establish trade relations. We have the option of exchanging commodities, or selling our goods for monetary value. All profit must be used to pay expenses and then be fully reinvested back into the community. I suggest it be used to buy land and property. Our lessons teach that the area of square miles of the planet earth is 196,940,000 square miles. And of this, the Original man uses 23 million square miles. All we need to form our own township is 36 square miles on a square tract of land 6 miles on each side. Let us deal with things in their proper order. Members of my community are quick to brag about how they get it "out the mud." If this is true then we should not lack the discipline needed to build it from the ground up. This is how we can begin to build the Kingdom of God. The Kingdom of God comes not through observation. The Kingdom of God comes from you looking within yourself and seeing what you can contribute to improve the world around you then you must show forth and prove your power by making your will manifest!

RAISING THE CITY WALLS WITH THE 12 JEWELS OF ISLAM

"The foundations of the wall of the city were adorned with all kinds of precious stones: the first foundation was jasper, the second sapphire, the third chalcedony, the fourth emerald, the fifth sardonyx, the sixth sardius, the seventh chrysolite, the eighth beryl, the ninth topaz, the tenth chrysoprase, the eleventh jacinth, and the twelfth amethyst." - Revelations 21:19-20

As the above verses reveal, the walls of the Kingdom of God are decorated with 12 gems or precious stones. Building a city with walls has become an outdated practice. So obviously this is not meant to be taken literally. It is allegorical and to properly interpret it we must view these passages using the culture of the men who wrote it. In the ancient world the walls of a city were the first line of defense. The city walls were a protective barrier keeping everything within their gates safe from all outside enemies. If your city walls could not be breached then your city could never be taken during an attack. As a result our ancestors would keep their most prized possessions hidden within their citadel's walls. The taller and stronger the walls were the better.

However, the walls that protect the Kingdom of God are adorn with jewels. 12 Jewels to be exact. This same symbolism is used in Exodus 28:17-21, the breastplate of the High Priest Aaron is also adorned with 12 precious jewels. A breastplate is a form of armor used to protect soldiers from attack. The imagery of something holy like a priest, or a city dedicated to God needing a city wall, or a breastplate to protect it from harm or attack is very revealing. It shows us that we have a duty to be diligent in defending ourselves and that which we love from the unrighteous. These weapons of war are associated with Godly images because they are both purely defensive. But on a deeper level it's not the breastplate or the wall that has the power to protect and defend. It is the jewels and the principles that they represent. The allegorical meaning of these 12 jewels also corresponds to the 12 tribes of Israel, and the 12 disciples. Each tribe/disciple has its corresponding zodiac sign, and each zodiac sign has a corresponding birthstone. And as intriguing as that may be, that will not be the focus of this discussion. The purpose of this writing is to instruct future generations on how to fulfill prophecy. Therefore, I must focus on the more practical aspects of the allegory's hidden meaning.

As I previously stated the purpose of a city having walls was to keep the things within the walls safe from outside threats. However, built within the walls of the Kingdom of God are the 12 Jewels Of Islam. These 12 principles are the protective barrier of defense that will protect us from all external threats.

THE 12 JEWELS OF ISLAM

1)Knowledge
2)Wisdom
3)Understanding
4)Freedom
5)Justice
6)Equality
7)Food
8)Clothing
9)Shelter

10)Love
11)Peace
12)Happiness

You need: 1) *Knowledge*, 2) *Wisdom*, and 3) *Understanding* before you can acquire 4) *Freedom*, 5) *Justice*, and 6) *Equality*. Once you begin thinking like your nation is equal with all others you will begin behaving like it is. This will compel you to start providing 7) *Food*, 8) *Clothing*, and 9) *Shelter* for your own selves. This is the only way to show and prove you 10) *Love* yourself and kind. Without this we will have no 11) *Peace*. But the moment we stop waiting for other nations to do for us what we have the power to do for self we will finally achieve lasting 12) *Happiness* as a nation of people.

We must stand firm on what we know to be true about White America. We cannot afford to continue to operate on our hopes or beliefs that they will one day treat us better when we have over 464 years of 1) *Knowledge* at our disposal. From John Hawkins tricking our ancestors to board his ship in 1555 to the false prophet politicians and anti-Christ who promised us the beast of mass incarceration would make the world a better place for us all. We must exercise 2) *Wisdom* or sound judgment by learning from the mistakes we've made in the past. 3) *Understanding* is the best part, because it brings clarity to the situation so that we may have the mental resolve needed to follow through. 4) *Freedom* is for those who think like they're free. 5) *Justice* and racial 6) *Equality* will always elude those who possess that old slave mentality. 7) *Food*, 8) *Clothing*, and 9) *Shelter* are the basic necessities of life, and you cannot survive without them. Knowledge of self teaches you how to 10) *Love* yourself so that you will gain the inner 11) *Peace* we all

97

yearn, and true 12) *Happiness* can only be achieved after the first 11 jewels have been acquired.

GEMSTONES AND THEIR PROPERTIES

Gemstones are beautiful and rare minerals that are sometimes worn as jewelry or as ornaments. Gemstones are formed in a variety of different ways. Some derive from igneous rocks, which require intense heat. These gemstones usually form from volcanic magma that has cooled. Others are generated from metamorphic rocks which undergo great pressure and heat. And lastly, there is sedimentary rocks.These gemstones originate from gravel or sand.

By understanding the process of how these jewels are made we can grasp the deeper meaning of the allegory. None of these gems can be gained easily, you have to mine the Earth (or dig deep within self) to reach them. This makes them rare. The difficulty in which they are made makes them precious. We as a nation of people have also been through these same intense conditions. The magma or hellfire the White race has put our people through. The intense pressure of living in a society that forces you to conform and assimilate to standards that you can never achieve due to your outward appearance. And the way they marginalize you and treat you like dirt when you can't. This explains our struggle as Blacks living in America perfectly. However, even the gravel and sand has an inner beauty that cannot be denied. All you have to do is polish it long enough and it too will shine with a natural brilliance. This is what the Nation of Gods and Earths was founded for. It was manifested to teach those whom America treated like dirt to polish themselves, and when enough of us began to shine then we would know that the walls of the city were now ready to be raised.

PROTECT AND DEFEND

Not all minerals can be gems. A mineral must possess a level of toughness and durability before it will be considered to be a gem. Mineralogist use the method of Mohs scale to measure a mineral's toughness. The scale ranges from 1 to 10 with 10 being the toughest. To be classified as a gem, the mineral must be rated a 7 or more. This is also very informative. By listing which type of gemstone each of the 12 Jewels are, our ancestors were also informing us of the toughness of that section of the city's wall. Only diamonds are rated 10 so this tells us that none of these defenses will make us immune from attack. No section of the walls protecting the Kingdom of God are impenetrable. But they don't have to be.

If they were perfect tens then this would mean we could slack off. But this is not the case at all. God's work is never done and once you gain these jewels you will have to defend them if you wish to keep them. Our ancestors built their city walls and then they posted guards to watch over them and defend them against attack. The 12 Jewels of Islam are the guards watching over our city walls. When you have 1) *Knowledge* that wall will one day come under attack from those speaking false knowledge. The wall guarded by 2) *Wisdom* will be targeted by foolishness. Misunderstanding will attack the section being defended by 3) *Understanding*. Those who wish to remain slaves will betray the weak points of the wall under the protection of 4) *Freedom*. 5) *Justice* will come under assault from those who wish to continue to treat those within your city

99

unjustly. Inequality will always attempt to tear down the wall being guarded by 6) *Equality*. Famine and drought will try to burrow underneath the wall being guarded by 7) *Food*. Extreme weather will frustrate 8) *Clothing* and 9) *Shelter's* ability to adequately protect their respective walls. 10) *Love* will constantly find its wall under siege by hate. 11) *Peace* will have to fend off chaos, and 12) *Happiness* will have to overcome the ambush of misery.

With that being said, another important point we cannot afford to overlook is the necessity of ensuring that we have access to a clean water supply. What took place in Flint, Michigan was environmental racism. The White power structure used environmental conditions to harm the Original people and they tried to cover it up. Then when they could no longer deny the truth, they justified it by saying using polluted lake water was necessary to save the city money. For those of you living in financially struggling municipalities I suggest you pay attention. White America has once again showed you that protecting the health and welfare of you and your children does not come before their priority to protect their bottom line.

I advise that we look into some of the methods used by some inhabitants of islands. If you lived on an island surrounded by salt water what do you do if there is no running tap water or you don't have access to bottled water? How would you supply your population with potable drinking water? We need to find ways of collecting and storing fresh rain water. In addition to this we also need to look at some of the impoverished nations of the world and learn from their misfortune. When water supplies become contaminated with harmful bacteria instead of lead, the effects of using untreated water can be even more dangerous. Cholera and Typhoid fever can be fatal. Therefore we need to make sure we have access to water treatment chemicals, or we must boil our stored drinking water before ingestion. There may be some who underestimate the wisdom of such advice, you're probably thinking you can just buy all the bottled water you need from the grocery store. However, in emergency situations there are two commodities that will be in short supply, and their prices have a tendency to increase during these occasions. They are water and gas. You and your family will not be the only ones who need water, and trying to purchase it at the last minute can become expensive. But why pay for what you can get for free?

I know that things will get better for the Original people in the future but we still need to prepare for the worst. We need to acquire the 12 jewels so that we will be able to protect ourselves for the tribulations that have yet to come. What makes rain, hail, snow and Earthquakes? All of the above are caused by the Sun of Man and the extreme weather patterns that will be unleashed are divine chastisement. Although it is intended for the unrighteous, there are casualties in war, and people do die from friendly fire when they are not doing what they're supposed to be doing. The Earth is not a pacifist. It possesses the ability to protect itself from all threats, even White Supremacy. The Sun is the most violent thing in our entire solar system. The violent collisions occurring between particles of gas within the Sun's core and the explosive power that causes plasma to be expelled from it put the planets under constant attack from solar flares and radioactive energy. However, only the Earth possessed the ability to defend itself from this constant bombardment. The layers of the atmosphere is how it defends itself against all threats both external and internal. This is why the allegory uses the imagery of the New

Jerusalem descending from heaven. The weather will be used as a weapon against them but the 12 jewels built within the city walls will protect and defend the righteous who use them to take refuge.

All 12 of the gemstones are natural and are merely different expressions of the Earth's natural beauty. The history of the Nation of Gods and Earths reveals that we associate the Black woman's nature to the planet Earth. The question of whether the Black woman was God was brought to Allah and his right hand man Justice Cee. Allah said that the Black woman was not a God but she was a Goddess. (But most Goddesses have Earth or lunar qualities, so we just call our women Earth.) But Justice Cee jokingly remarked that some of the females were more God than the Gods. The 12 jewels are just minerals of the Earth that possess a certain strength and rare quality about them. In my opinion the most valuable gem is the natural beauty of a strong Black woman of integrity.

RELATIONSHIPS AND UNDERSTANDING THE VALUE OF A GEM

The value of the gem is determined by a variety of factors—cut, clarity, color, weight, and rarity. The cutting of the gemstone is a precise science. If it is not done correctly then you may fracture the stone and distort it's clarity. You cannot cut a gem with a weaker gem. The gem must be of equal hardness or greater. This also applies to relationships between Gods and their Earths. A weak man cannot mold a strong woman. You must be her equal in mental toughness or greater. Otherwise any attempt to cut the gem will not work. Your woman will show you she is "more God" than you. Foolish women despise self-improvement but wise women will embrace it. However, you must be careful that you do not fracture the relationship by abusing her trust. She is entrusting you to guide her in the right direction. Any cut made permits the gem to absorb light and slow it down. The more light a gem can slow down the more brilliant it shines. Likewise, the cuts you make to the character of your women should also permit her to interact with your light more effectively. The knowledge you share with her is the light that you give, and this light should bring out her best qualities allowing her to shine more brilliantly as any gem should. When this occurs within a gem the light rays are bending as they bounce around the inside of the gem. This is called refraction.

Nowadays the trend is to act as though we can no longer see color. However, when appreciating any gem the color is vital to its beauty, value and splendor. You cannot use color to determine the type of gem. Similarly, you cannot use color to determine a woman's nationality either. Many nations of people share the same color just as gems do. Thus, gems and women are sometimes indistinguishable when determining their value by color alone. Yet, there are many indoctrinated Black men who only like light skinned women or White women. You can have your own personal preference for what you like. But it's important to understand why you have these preferences. The U.S. Census report reveals that the Black woman is the least likely person in America to get married and that the Black man in America is the mostly likely to marry someone outside of his own race. This is problematic, because if there is no unity between Black men and Black women then we cannot overcome the effects of White supremacy. Marriage may not be for everyone, and for others we may feel like we do not need our enslavers' government to validate the love we have for our women. But for those Blacks who are not opposed to getting married, why are some eligible Black men more likely to commit to White women? It is because they are judging a gems value by the color alone, and they're indoctrination leads them to believe the lighter the gem is the more valuable it is. Natural gems come in a variety of different shades and colors. The Nation of Gods and Earths does not value any particular shade of the Original woman over the others. The Black, Brown and Yellow are all viewed as equals. They are each a different expression of the same gene type.

What is the total weight of the planet Earth? Is it really 6 sextillion tons? The value of rare gems is also determined by the number of carats. One carat equals 0.007 ounces or 0.2 grams. The more carats a gem has this can also increase its value. So we now reach the question, "how much of a gem is your woman?" Are you measuring her physical features, her integrity, or is it a combination of both? The amount of carats corresponds to a woman's integrity. However, the specific gravity of a gem corresponds to her physical features. The specific gravity deals with the density of the gem's crystals. Each type of gemstone has a specific gravity, and you can measure it by comparing an equal volume or weight of the gem to an equal ratio of pure water. A diamond weighs about 3.5 times as much as an equal volume of pure water. How does this correspond to the Black woman you ask?

In ancient Egyptian Mythology, the deceased would have to stand before Ma'at the Goddess of justice and righteousness. The test to determine if you were worthy enough to make it into "heaven" was that your heart would be placed on a scale and weighed in comparison to a feather. If the heart was heavier than the feather then it was determined that you lived an unrighteous life and you would be denied entry. The specific gravity or the density of the planet Earth's mass is 6 sextillion tons. However, if you could place the Earth (both the planet and the righteous Black woman) on Ma'at's scale and weigh either against that feather they both will be judged to have lived a pure life. Because like everything else in space the planet is actually weightless. This allegorical story shows that the Egyptians understood the way physics worked both on the Earth and in the heavens above. The carats of a gem, like a woman's integrity, are important factors in determining it's value. The specific gravity, like a woman's physical features, only measure mass. The Black man has a responsibility to teach the unrefined Black woman civilization, righteousness, the knowledge of herself and the science of everything in life, which is love, peace and happiness. When this has been accomplished carrying the weight of the world becomes no burden at all.

The last component of appraisal is the rarity of the gem. I was once told a story about a conversation Muhammad Ali had with one of his daughters. I cannot verify the truthfulness of this story. But it serves as a useful teaching tool nonetheless: The story goes that Muhammad Ali noticed that one of his daughters was not wearing her hijab. The hijab is the head covering worn by Muslim women and girls. So Muhammad Ali called his daughter to him and sat her on his lap. He asked the girl why she was not wearing the hijab and his daughter then responded that she did not like wearing it. Muhammad Ali asked her did she understand why he wanted her to wear it and the importance of her keeping her body covered? The little girl did not. So it is said that Muhammad Ali told her, "You are a precious gem and precious gems are not easily gained. Men must mine and go deep within the Earth before they can uncover it's treasures. You must keep your body covered because you my daughter are one of those treasures. The things that are commonly gazed upon by men are not valued or respected by them."

In the Nation of Gods and Earths our women are taught to keep 3/4ths of their bodies covered when in public. The 3/4ths symbolizes the ratio of water covering the Earth's surface. The 8th jewel of the 12 Jewels Of Islam is clothing. The 8th precious stone on the city wall is beryl. Beryl is an igneous rock which means it is formed from volcanic activity. I can imagine there are many Black women who will erupt if you were to tell them you wanted them to keep their bodies covered. But from this eruption and intensely heated conversation a very important gem will form when the Earth cools. It is through nakedness that the White power structure is successfully attacking us. His portrayal of Black women as whores are convincing and extremely effective. What sensible self respecting man wants to marry a whore? The lustful nature of a man will cause him to desire to lay with her, but very few of us want to take you home to meet our mothers. This hyper sexualization of the Black woman's image is not as progressive as Black women have been led to believe. If it is then why are you the only ones being predominantly portrayed in such a light? Yet, you wonder why respectable Black men are committing themselves to more wholesome images. You think you are being sexually liberated when really, you are being sexually ensnared. Are you too blind to see that the world is struggling to look at you as being more than just an object of sexual desire. I do not agree with this view of women and I am not suggesting this is the case for all women. There are exceptions to every rule. Neither am I suggesting that women are too weak or helpless to do something to change this. You can change it by keeping your body covered. And the next time you choose to reveal your nakedness to a man he will value it for the rare treasure it is.

"We do not inherit the world from our parents, we borrow it from our children."
—*Native American Proverb*

It's been said that we should plant seeds that will grow into trees whose shade we shall never enjoy. This is how you accumulate generational wealth. As Black men and Women we have to find ways to invest into Black children's future. I know you will grow to appreciate this knowledge being preserved for you so that you would have access to it when the time was right. This is my contribution and deposit toward making the world we live in a better place for you who are the rightful owners of it. I hope that these words motivate you to also pick the pen up and begin writing your own history in advance. From the 1st Qur'an to the last, the cipher shows and proves the future is destined to look like the past. All praise due to you, because the babies are the greatest. Apotheosis is the elevation or exaltation of a person to the rank of God, and the True and Living is the ideal example or epitome of Godhood. Peace Young Gods and Young Earths!

P.E.A.C.E

Political Economic And Community Elevation

AFTERWORD

With such a divisive leader in the highest seat in office the U.S. seems to be moving dangerously close to another civil war. Civil wars are the deadliest and bloodiest of all wars. More American lives were lost in the first Civil War than all other wars including both World Wars. Although the Muller Report exonerated President Trump of collusion, it did not exonerate him of obstruction. However, Muller determined that he could not charge a sitting president with a crime, therefore, Muller declined to make a criminal accusation out of respect for the office. However, Muller did note that this executive immunity only lasts while Trump remains in office. But he stated that Trump can still be impeached by Congress.

The speaker of the House Nancy Pelosi has gone on record stating that she does not support impeachment because the country is so divided. Why would Congresswoman Pelosi be afraid to hold a bigot like Trump accountable? Because she realizes that this move would play right into the hands of Trump and his base. It is no secret that the weakness of democracy is that it can deteriorate into rule by mob, and that this will deteriorate into a dictatorship. The election of the 2008 Democratic nominee to the highest seat in office ignited a fervor into the White race. Witnessing a Black man by the name of Barack Obama, become President of the United States, and then serve an eight year term, evoked a hatred in White America that many of us hadn't seen since the Civil Rights era. This racism that had been covert up until then, was now overt, and this White backlash resulted in Trump usurping the Good Old Boys Party (GOP) as a renegade Republican, and the White mob who appointed him now gives him license to override the U.S. Constitution (so that he may govern this nation as its absolute ruler) and restore order by putting the minorities back in their place.

So when Congresswoman Pelosi says she is against impeaching Trump, it is not because obstruction fails to meet the threshold of being an impeachable offense; it is only because she is trying to avoid being baited into instigating a civil war. But by not holding President Trump accountable, Congress will also be setting a new precedent - that the President IS above the law. But I'm of the opinion that if Trump fails to get re-elected for a second term, he will rile up his base by alleging voter fraud and incite them to revolt anyway. For you who are too blind to understand the signs of the time, let me direct your attention to the case of Lt. Christopher Hasson, an officer in the National Guard and a proud White Supremacist. Hasson was arrested and caught with a stockpile of weapons, and a review of his browser history revealed that he had did searches on which guns would be most effective in killing Blacks, and he had visited a White Nationalist website that promoted the idea that to impeach Trump would start the Civil War.

Therefore, there seems to be a strong possibility that we are on the fringes of a constitutional crisis, and that another civil war may be inevitable. So the question now becomes how should Blacks respond? It is my personal opinion that all Black people should sit this one out. Let the White people kill each other if that's what they want to do. Why should we fight on their front lines where the fighting will be the fiercest? Why should anymore Black parents send their Black children to take bullets for a White power structure that oppresses them? Do they really expect our men and women to serve in their military when they have people like Lt. Christopher Hasson in their ranks? I'm sure both sides will promise us reparations and the coveted 40 acres and a mule. But they both made these same promises during the last Civil War, and look how far that has gotten us. So why should we believe that this time will be any different? We have no reason to believe that either side will honor their word. So yes, I say when the fighting breaks out, Black man make yourself hard to find. Take your women and children somewhere safe and hold down your own fort for a change, and exercise the 3rd Amendment by refusing to give quarters to both the Yankee and the Dixie. Let them know what it feels like to be abandoned by their fellow American for a change. Don't worry about them hating you for it. They've been hating us for over four hundred years anyway, so that's nothing new.

When the next civil war breaks out Black people must be ready when the looting and plundering begin. Instead of stealing TV's and stereos, I expect Black people will be wise enough to stake their claim to some land. And I think that they would be well within their rights to defend that plot and parcel with tooth and nail against whoever seeks to occupy it without their consent. We do not need to overthrow your government to form our own nation. All we have to do is wait and when revolt and sedition causes you to suspend your own constitution, then natural law once again becomes the law of the land. When this occurs, our goal should be to assert our independence as a nation of people separate and distinct from their government. In order to get our nation universally recognized as an independent state, we must have land, we need a flag, we need a name to proclaim as our nationality. Black people in America have an overabundance of all of the above. But what we have yet to establish is that we have acquired the means to govern ourselves, that we can feed ourselves and lastly, but most importantly, that we can defend ourselves. Until we can do these things sufficiently, we are doomed to remain in subjugation as a conquered people. Black people don't owe any loyalty to the Yankee or Dixie. Therefore, we shouldn't choose any side at all. With the recent Black face scandals involving Virginia's Governor Ralph Northam and Virginia's Attorney General Mark Herring, it should be clear to Black people that the Democratic party is just as racist as it was during the antebellum period, reconstruction period, Jim Crow period, and Civil Rights period. Let it be known that for the Black man in America, the more things have changed, in reality, the more that they have really remained the same.

Thus, I will conclude this appeal with this: there is much talk about the progress Blacks have made in the U.S. but you cannot accurately measure progress by time alone. Progress, specifically the topic of Black progress, is a measurement of distance. We must measure our previous position as a race against where our feet stand today. But it doesn't stop there. Next, we must determine if our current position is the destination that our ancestors desired for us? If the answer is "no", then we must measure the distance from where we stand today, so that we may accurately determine how much further we still must go.

Both the integrationist and nationalist believed Blacks needed the protection of a nation. One believed we could depend on the U.S. to protect us, while the other believed we had to build a separate nation of our own. It is clear that the U.S. government is not protecting us, yet, we still don't have our own government either. Until we have achieved nationhood as a people any celebration of Black progress, in my opinion, is premature. Compare the images of Black children being assaulted by White police during sit ins and marches to the image of Lucca being pepper sprayed, body slammed to the ground, punched in the back of the head and then having his head slammed into the concrete by a White cop. I have one question for you - Tell me America, where do you see the progress in that?

Lord Serious Hakim Allah, 120°+

P.E.A.C.E.
Praising Every Ancestor's Contribution Equally

Declaration of Black National Independence

When a group of people, so long enslaved by another, begin their destined trek down the road to liberty, there inevitably comes a time at which these travelers must rid themselves of the political bonds that once tied them to another, and take hold of the separate and equal station, bequeathed them at birth, by their Mother Nature and Father God. Upon arrival at such destination, wisdom dictates that such a group must, for the sake of humanity, state plainly and truly the course of events that have brought them to such a station.

We hold these truths to be self-evident that all men are created equal; that they are endowed by their creator with certain unalienable rights; that among these are life, liberty, and the pursuit of happiness; that, to secure these rights governments are instituted among people, deriving their just powers from the consent of the governed; that whenever any form of government becomes destructive of these ends, it is the right of the people—of ALL people—to alter or abolish it, and to create for themselves a new government, laying its foundation on such principles, and organizing its powers in such form, as to them shall seem most likely to effect their safety, happiness, and prosperity. Prudence, indeed, will dictate that governments long established should not be changed for light and transient causes and accordingly all experience has shown that people are more inclined to suffer, while evils are sufferable, than to right themselves by abolishing the forms to which they are accustomed. But when a long train of abuses and usurpations, pursuing invariably the same object, exposes a system designed to reduce them under absolute domination, it is their right, it is their duty and obligation, to throw off such government and to provide new guards for their future. Such has been the patient sufferance of America's Black Colony and as such is now the necessity which forces them to alter their former political relationship. The history of the present United States of America is a history of repeated injuries and oppression, all having in direct object the establishment of an absolute supremacy over its Black Colonies. To prove this, let these facts be submitted to a candid world:

History records that America's Black Colonies are made up of an aggregation of men, women and children—descendants of the African continent—stolen from our native lands and transported to this country; forced to suffer conditions not fit for the lowliest of beasts; causing the deaths of millions of men, women and children during what has come to be known as the Atlantic Slave Trade;

For over 200 years, members of the Black Colony were relegated to the legal status of slaves and made to suffer rape, molestation, brutally savage beatings, quarterings, castrations, hangings, burnings, whippings, murders, and a host of other atrocious acts, all sanctioned by the American government;

To justify the barbarity of the slave system, the corresponding myths of White Supremacy and Black Inferiority were created and propagated through every institution in America;

The Compromise of 1877, allowing for the withdrawal of federal troops from an openly racist South, would lead to a set of laws and decrees known as Jim Crow, designed to isolate, subordinate and degrade members of the Black Colony while simultaneously retarding any progress made towards equality through systematic segregation and discrimination in all areas of people activity, guaranteeing our second class status;

It has adamantly denied any monetary compensation (or other form of reparations) for the horrors endured by past victims of the slavery system and Jim Crow era, nor has it substantially addressed the impact that such a legacy has had on current members of the Black Colony;

It has created, substantiated and propagated a legacy of poverty for members of the Black Colony through unjust laws and policies;

It has created racially segregated ghettos for its undesired Black Colony, filling these ghettos with guns, alcohol and addictive narcotics, purposefully encouraging its inhabitants to engage in suicidal acts of genocide;

It has deliberately and intentionally kept the children of the Black Colony under-educated and misinformed through its racially segregated, underfunded and unequal public school system;

Its social welfare program promotes and encourages the destruction of the Black family unit;

It maintains and supports the illusion of White Supremacy and Black Inferiority through its teaching of a whitewashed interpretation of history;

Its media has engaged in a propaganda campaign, disproportionately depicting male members of the Black Colony as dangerous and violent thugs, criminals, gangsters, etc.; turning the public against us and promoting the continuously "justified" and sanctioned murders of young black men— whether armed or unarmed;

Its "Jezebel" portrayal of Black women has been used to justify a hyper-sexual objectification and mistreatment of female members of the Black Colony;

Its centuries of mental, physical and spiritual abuse has severely damaged the collective psyche of the Black Colony, leading to high rates of self-hate, depression and inferiority complexes among its members;

Its sanctioned agents have consistently committed unjust killings of members of the Black Colony that their courts have judged as lawful and justified;

It has used its power of influence to disrupt any large business dealings that advocates of the Black Colony have sought to enter into with other sovereign nations, restricting us in trade and commerce;

It has deliberately and strategically fractured and kept divided our national leadership and diplomatic relationships with other nations in order to protect "U.S. interest";

Its agents have consistently murdered, or sanctioned the murder of, any male member of the Black Colony that displays the power to bring about substantial change in the social dynamic; instilling fear into the hearts and minds of subsequent generations, effectively paralyzing our liberation efforts;

It has branded our liberation groups and community protection programs as "domestic terrorists" and sent its agents to infiltrate, disrupt and/or destroy our organizing efforts;

It has intentionally retarded the growth of Black Business through violent acts of intimidation and terror, race-based and biased legislation, and a lack of proper prosecution for discriminatory practices;;

It has constrained our fellow members of the Black Colony— having taken them captive in their courts, classrooms and corporations— to work against their people and become oppressors of their friends and family or to themselves suffer as victims of the system;

The agents of this government have consistently used their power of office to enact unjust legislation and to prevent any substantial change in their relations with the Black Colony;

Its Supreme Court has consistently upheld the racial bias in the country; having once ruled that "the black man has no rights that the white man is bound to respect";

It has allowed its states to continuously pass laws that have a disproportionately negative effect on the Black Colony;

It has obstructed the administration of justice by maintaining police forces that do not reflect the demographic or cultural makeup of the area in which they are stationed, nor that live in the bounds of said area, essentially quartering is law enforcement officers in our communities;

It has, for the last 30 years, increasingly militarized its police force, turning its cops into soldiers who patrol our communities day and night; harassing, terrorizing and in all other ways disturbing inhabitants, as if engaged in the occupational stages of war;

Its agents have deliberately poured, or allowed to enter, large volumes of addictive narcotics into our communities, initiating a long-term plan of chemical warfare that has devastated the relations among our own;

Under former Presidents Richard Nixon and Ronald Reagan, a domestic war on the Black Colony was waged under the guise of a War On Drugs that has decimated the Black Colony; beginning in the late 1970s and continually now for over 30 years;

In response to the masses of poor, uneducated and out of work members of the Black Colony's engagement in criminal activities to survive, a policy of mass incarceration has been enacted; focused on warehousing and punishing violators rather than aiding or rehabilitating them;

Using its biased justice system's "felon" brand, the system has disenfranchised a large mass of the Black Colony, while still requiring these so-called citizens (with no voting rights) to pay taxes and be subject to their laws;

Using the "felon" brand, many males in the Black Colony have also been denied their constitutional right to bear arms, leaving them powerless to defend themselves, their families or their property;

Its state officials have contractually promised the sadistic builders of prisons Black bodies to fill their beds; bodies that have been made "criminal" to create and secure jobs for its White rural agents; simultaneously robbing our communities of their people's human potential;

It has shown a determined reluctance to abolish White Supremacy in substance; craftily preserving the system through cosmetic transformations and repeated denial of its existence;

It has committed crimes against our very bodies, forcibly injecting us with various biological entities throughout the years, using us like lab rats for their inhumane experiments;

It has suppressed the knowledge and wisdom of our ancient cultures and usurped our heritage, forcing members of the Black Colony to live in a way contrary to the will of our Father God and Mother Nature.

In every stage of these oppressions we have petitioned for redress in the most humblest of terms; our repeated petitions have been answered only by repeated injury. A government, whose character is thus stained by every act which may define depression, is unfit to rule over and govern a naturally free people.

Nor have we been wanting in our attention to our American brethren. We have warned them time after time of the horrors of oppression that they inflict upon us daily. We have marched in the streets; we have protesting in front of a logical and rational world, making our case plane for all eyes to see; we have spoken out in their journals, their newspapers, on television programs and radio shows, stood in the pulpits and on soap boxes, and even debated in the legislative halls; but yet, still, our voices have gone ignored. We have reminded them of the inevitable result of such conditioning upon our children and future generations. We have appealed to their native justice and compassion; and we have beseeched them, by the ties of our common humanity, to disavow this stifling climate of oppression. They, too, have been deaf to the voice of justice and brotherhood. We must, therefore, acquiesce in the face of Truth, in the necessity which denounces our separation and declares our liberty, and hold them, as we hold the rest of mankind, enemies in war, in peace friends.

We, therefore, the representatives of this United Black Nation, in heart, mind and body, appealing to the Supreme Judge of the Universe for the rectitude of our intentions, do, in the name and by the authority of the good people of this Colony, solemnly publish and declare, that the Black Colony is, and of right ought to be, a FREE and INDEPENDENT Nation; that it is absolved from all allegiance to the United States of America and that all political connection between it and the United States of America is and ought to be totally dissolved; and that, as a free and independent nation they have full power to levy war, conclude peace, contrast alliances, establish commerce, and do all the acts and things independent nations may of right do. And for the support of this declaration, with a firm reliance on the protection of Universal Law, we mutually pledge to each other our lives our fortunes and our sacred honor.

—Saint Sincere Quintessence Allah (Q. Jones III) 120°+

Black family I ask: Would you be willing to sign your name to this document?

Eventually there must come a point when we stop begging our oppressors for freedom and realize that power is never given to the powerless; it must be taken.

"[The] struggle may be a moral one, or maybe a physical one, or maybe both moral and physical, but it must be a struggle. Power concedes nothing without a demand. It never did and it never will. Find out what people will submit to and you have found the exact measure of injustice and wrong which would be impressed upon them, and these will continue till they all resisted with either words or blows, or with both. The limits of the tyrants are prescribed by the endurance of those whom they oppress."

—Frederick Douglass

P.E.A.C.E.
Proper Education
Always Corrects Errors

About The Author

Lord Serious Hakim Allah was born James R. Boughton Jr. After being sentenced to 38 years and six months in prison he has now written a first hand account on the enslavement of Blacks during the 21st Century, and what must be done to overcome White supremacy and mass incarceration. Lord Serious has been incarcerated since he was 19 years old. However, the time spent in physical bondage soon led to his mental freedom when a fellow prisoner introduced him to the Nation of Gods and Earths. After gaining the knowledge of self, Lord Serious realized that his life had a greater purpose. His first book, The Powerless Pinky, was published in 2019, and The Five Percenter Newspaper gave this children's book a 5-star rating.

www.ingramcontent.com/pod-product-compliance
Lightning Source LLC
Chambersburg PA
CBHW050354280326
41933CB00010BA/1466